Discover AI in the Real World

No Skill Needed to Demystify Machine
Learning, Explore Everyday AI Tools,
and Ethically Leverage Generative AI
for Work, Family, and Future-Ready
Skills

George Munson

GL Digital Publishing LLC

GEORGE MUNSON

First Edition 2025

For my daughter, Nora...
Thank you for your never-ending help!
Love, Dad

Contents

Introduction

A few months ago, I found myself juggling three different projects, two books in development, and a dozen email notifications pinging on my phone from potential designers. It's a familiar scene. A single nudge saved my day from my digital calendar: "Meeting with designer in 15 minutes." That gentle reminder, powered by artificial intelligence, brought a sense of relief amidst the chaos, keeping a critical conversation from slipping through the cracks. Later that week, a chatbot at my bank sorted out a payment issue in less time than it took to make a cup of coffee. I barely noticed the technology at work, but it made everything run more smoothly in the background.

That's what this book is about: the small, meaningful ways AI can help you every day. You don't have to speak in code, know complex math, or work in tech to make AI work for you. This book will show you how to turn artificial intelligence into your assistant at home, at work, and everywhere in between. If you've ever felt overwhelmed by all the hype or worried that AI is just for big companies and computer experts, you're not alone. My goal is simple: by the end of this book, you'll see how AI can make your life easier, your work more productive, and your future a little brighter, no matter your background or experience. You'll feel empowered and capable, ready to take on the AI revolution.

Why am I so passionate about this? Because, like you, I've been frustrated by new technology that promises the world but delivers confusion, wasted time, and more stress. I've seen competent adults, parents, teachers, business owners, and busy professionals who feel left out or anxious about keeping up with the demands of their roles. I wrote this book for you. I want to strip away the myths, the jargon, and the pressure, and give you real, honest answers. I want you to feel confident, not lost, when people talk about AI.

Let's address those pain points for a moment. Information overload is real. Every day, we're hit with emails, messages, and news from every direction. Tool confusion is everywhere; there's always a new app, a new service, another "must-have" platform. AI hype is loud and often misleading. It's challenging to discern what's real, what works, and what truly matters. And then there are the big worries: Will I lose my job to a robot? Is AI spying on me? Is this technology even fair or ethical? If any of that sounds familiar, you're in the right place.

This book is designed to address these problems. It's a hands-on, practical guide. There's no coding required. No need to wade through thick technical manuals. You'll get honest explanations, clear instructions, and plenty of examples of how you can use AI today. You'll discover free tools and interactive resources to support you as you explore and try out new things. I've included real stories from people just like you, parents using AI to organize family life, teachers making lesson planning easier, and business owners saving hours on routine tasks.

What sets this book apart is its focus on you as a real person, not just a "user." You'll find step-by-step how-to guides, quick-start checklists, and frameworks for deciding what AI tools fit your life or work. There's also a whole section on ethics and emotional intelligence, as AI is about people, not just machines.

This book is for anyone who wants to get results, not just to read AI theory. Whether you're a parent, an educator, a professional, or running your own business, you'll find practical answers here. If you want to save time, reduce stress, and build skills for the future, you're in the right place.

You might worry that tech books get outdated fast. Or maybe you feel anxious that you'll get lost in technical talk, or that most guides only scratch the surface. I get it. That's why I built this book around real-world tasks, not abstract ideas. I'll bust the biggest myths about AI, and I'll be clear about what AI can and can't do right now.

Here's how the book is set up. We'll start by clearing up what AI is (and isn't), so you feel grounded from the start. Next, you'll learn about the best AI tools for your personal life, such as calendars, reminders, smart shopping, and more. Next, we'll move on to the workplace: how AI can assist with communication, organization, and creative tasks. Following that, there's a section for business owners explaining how AI can enhance your team, streamline customer service, and reduce repetitive work. We'll discuss ethics, emotional intelligence, and the significant questions surrounding trust and fairness. Finally, we'll look to the future, offering tips on building AI skills that'll keep you prepared for whatever comes next, including the potential impact of AI on jobs and society.

As you read, I invite you to treat this book like a hands-on companion. Try out the tools. Reflect on the prompts at the end of each chapter. Join the learning community and share your experiences. This book is not just reading about AI; it's about using it, shaping it, and growing with it. The interactive features and community aspect are designed to help you do just that.

If you've ever felt overwhelmed, confused, or just plain skeptical about AI, know that you're not alone. My goal is to support you, answer your fundamental questions, and help you make AI your assistant, starting today. Let's get started.

Chapter One

Demystifying AI for Foundations Without the Fear

Have you ever noticed how your phone seems to know what you need before you ask, such as suggesting quick email replies or rerouting your trip around unexpected traffic? These conveniences might feel like magic, but they're powered by artificial intelligence. When people hear the term "AI," they often envision sci-fi robots or machines with human-like intelligence. But AI isn't magic, nor is it about computers actually "thinking" like people. Instead, it's about recognizing patterns, making predictions, and sifting through vast amounts of data, like a tireless, ultra-organized assistant. This assistant doesn't understand or care about what's happening; it simply follows programmed rules. Understanding these practical applications of AI can make you feel more informed and aware of its real-world impact.

How Machines Really "Learn" and Why AI Isn't Magic

To start, AI is not mystical. It's built on algorithms, sets of rules, and immense amounts of data. Take your phone's autocomplete: it suggests your next word not by knowing you, but because it has analyzed countless messages and spotted which words usually follow others. It's a statistical prediction, not mind-reading. AI employs this approach everywhere, from recommending music and filtering emails to assisting doctors in identifying patterns in scans. The quality of the input matters so much because, as the adage goes, "garbage in, garbage out." Good data enables beneficial results; insufficient data leads to nonsense. Stressing the role of data in AI can make you appreciate its importance.

For AI, "learning" isn't like human learning. There are three main ways machines "learn":

- **Supervised learning:** This is like teaching by example. If you want a child to tell apples from oranges, you show labeled pictures—"apple," "orange"—until they can do it themselves. Similarly, AI uses labeled data (like tagged photos) to learn to make predictions.

- **Unsupervised learning:** This method finds patterns without labels. Imagine dumping vacation photos into a folder and asking the computer to organize them without any guidance. It might group beach scenes, mountain hikes, or city skylines by visual similarities, without any prior hints.

- **Reinforcement learning:** Here, learning comes through trial and error, like learning to ride a bike: you do better each time you avoid a fall. For AI, it tries things out and receives feedback—rewards for right moves, penalties for errors—improving gradually. Playing chess, it learns what leads to winning over thousands of games.

These systems rely on feedback loops, not intuition or wisdom. They measure progress using a "loss function," a type of scoreboard that indicates how close they are to the correct answer. Labeled data is crucial because it provides the machine with a reference point for verifying its predictions.

AI can seem impressive. It processes massive data at speeds humans never could, beats chess grandmasters, and can spot minuscule flaws in manufacturing. However, it's essential to remember that AI is "narrow": it excels at one specific skill when trained for it, but struggles when the task changes. Chess-playing AI can't tie shoelaces or catch sarcasm in a conversation. Human intelligence is broad and flexible; AI is specialized and rigid (Bennett, 2024). Even simple human tasks, such as walking into a cluttered room and identifying what's amiss, can stump even advanced AI. Emphasizing these limitations can make you feel cautious and critical about its capabilities.

Think of a repetitive or predictable task in your life (like sorting emails or planning a commute). How do you decide your next step? Write down your thought process. Could a computer follow those same steps if it had enough examples?

From Buzzwords to Basics: Decoding Machine Learning, Deep Learning, and NLP

Machine learning, deep learning, and natural language processing (NLP) are now ubiquitous, appearing in news headlines and workplace meetings. They are often grouped, but each has its distinct flavor. Machine learning is probably the one you've heard most. In plain English, it means teaching computers to make decisions or predictions using data, rather than giving them strict instructions. Think of a spam filter in your email inbox. Instead of coding every possible spam phrase, engineers feed the program thousands of examples, some of which are marked as spam, while others are marked as safe. Over time, the system recognizes patterns and starts making its own "educated guesses." If you've noticed your inbox getting cleaner over the years, that's machine learning at work behind the scenes.

Deep learning is a branch of machine learning, but with more layers, literally. Imagine peeling an onion: each layer reveals a deeper insight into the data, capturing more complex patterns. Deep learning models are made of artificial "neurons" stacked in layers (hence the term "deep"). This enables them to recognize faces in photos, pick out voices in a noisy environment, or identify objects in traffic camera feeds. When you unlock your phone with your face or ask Alexa to play a song, deep learning powers those features. It's not that deep means smarter; it just means the system can process more complicated information by stacking more layers together. These models require massive amounts of data and computing power, think millions of selfies or hours of audio recordings, to perform effectively.

Natural language processing (NLP) is all about computers under-standing and generating human language, our words, sentences, and even slang. Translation apps? That's NLP in action. Virtual assistants, such as Siri or Google Assistant, use NLP to convert your spoken commands into actions. When you dictate a text and your phone types what you say, that's NLP listening and interpreting. Even those pre-dictive text suggestions you see while texting stem from NLP models scanning your message for context and offering likely following words. However, don't expect miracles; NLP often struggles with sarcasm, idioms, and subtle humor.

These technologies aren't science fiction; they're in almost every app or service you use. Netflix uses machine learning algorithms to suggest movies based on what you've watched and liked. Spotify rec-ommends playlists using deep learning to analyze song features and user habits. Banks fight fraud by flagging unusual transactions with machine learning models trained on millions of customer histories. If you write emails in Gmail, notice how it suggests phrases as you type? That's a blend of NLP and machine learning, making your life easier.

Now, here's why all these buzzwords matter for everyday folks and not just techies in Silicon Valley: they shape your digital experiences constantly, sometimes invisibly. When you scroll through social media feeds, algorithms powered by these tools decide which posts you see first. When new apps roll out more innovative features seemingly overnight, such as instant translation in messaging or lightning-fast photo sorting, it's often because of a phenomenon called "transfer learning." This means that AI models trained on massive tasks (such as recognizing cats and dogs) are tweaked to perform new jobs (like identifying specific dog breeds) with less effort. This leads to rapid improvements for users, eliminating the need to wait years for new inventions.

A few misconceptions need clearing up, though. Deep learning isn't automatically "better" because it's deeper. More layers mean more potential to recognize complex features, but also a greater chance for mistakes or confusion if the data isn't plentiful or clean. Deep learning requires robust hardware and substantial amounts of labeled data; without these, it won't impress anyone. NLP isn't the same as translation; it encompasses everything from understanding sentiment in product reviews to summarizing long articles, transcribing speech to text, and more. However, even the most advanced NLP models still struggle with context, sarcasm, or double meanings, things that most children grasp easily.

Large Language Models Explained as the Brains Behind ChatGPT and Beyond

Imagine your phone's autocomplete on steroids, suggesting not just the next word but entire paragraphs, drawing from a vast library of texts. That's how large language models (LLMs) operate: as ultra-advanced autocompletes trained on billions of words sourced from books, websites, articles, and online conversations. Rather than simply recalling your messages, these models use their training to mimic how humans write and speak closely. When you chat with ChatGPT, you're essentially interacting with a system that predicts the most likely next word or sentence, aiming to sound convincingly human, not because it "understands," but because it excels at juggling probabilities.

LLMs derive their power from massive datasets, encompassing everything from recipe blogs to classic literature. They analyze this content to build a statistical map of how language works, including which words often pair, how sentences unfold, and what usually follows specific questions, among other things. Rather than knowing facts, LLMs identify and replicate patterns. When you give a prompt, the model breaks your input into tokens (units of meaning), picks the most probable following tokens, and strings them together. The larger and more diverse the data it's trained on, the more fluent and adaptable its responses. However, any bias or error in the original data gets embedded in the model's behavior.

How you phrase your prompt matters a great deal; this is known as "prompt engineering." Try asking, "Give me a quick dinner idea with chicken and broccoli," versus, "What's a healthy meal I can make with chicken and broccoli in under 20 minutes?" The answers shift depending on the detail and focus of your request. Even bigger changes occur with broader prompts, such as "Write me a business plan for an online bakery," compared to something more targeted, like "Draft a five-step marketing plan for selling cupcakes online to college students." The more guidance you provide, the more tailored the model's output becomes. Prompt engineering is like giving directions to someone who knows every street in town but needs clarity on your destination.

LLMs are especially effective at specific tasks, such as summarizing lengthy content, generating lists or brainstorming ideas, and producing first drafts for a wide range of applications, from greeting cards to business proposals. They process information quickly and handle repetitive requests with ease. Still, they have notable downsides: sometimes LLMs fabricate information, and these so-called "hallucinations" can mean invented facts, sources, or confidently wrong answers. For example, they might offer plausible but inaccurate medical advice or misinterpret sarcasm, complex humor, or subtle emotional cues. Biases, reflecting stereotypes or mistakes found in their training sources, can also appear in LLMs' output (Nature Humanities and Social Sciences Communications, 2024).

If LLMs seem bright but not truly intelligent, that's accurate. These models don't actually "think" or grasp meaning; they're sophisticated parrots, copying language patterns without real understanding or reasoning. They don't draw on genuine experience; instead, they predict likely following words based on earlier patterns. Just as a well-trained parrot might deliver the perfect phrase or complete nonsense, LLMs sometimes sound spot-on and other times miss the mark entirely. Human experts, in contrast, understand the meaning and context behind words. Remember, LLMs are advanced tools that are helpful, but not infallible. Always verify their outputs, especially when facts or accuracy are at stake.

A Prompt Experiment

Try these two prompts with any major chatbot (*ChatGPT, Gemini,* etc.):

- "Tell me how to write a short story."

- "Write a 300-word short story about a lost dog who finds its owner."

- Note how the responses differ, especially when your request is more specific.

Separating Hype from Everyday Use, an AI Reality Check

Myth-busting has never been more critical than it is with artificial intelligence, and nowhere is the noise louder than the claim, "AI will take all jobs." You've probably read headlines predicting a future where robots run every store, write every article, and drive every truck. The truth is far less dramatic. AI automates specific tasks, often the most repetitive or data-heavy ones, but not entire professions. Consider your most recent online customer support chat. The first line of help was likely a chatbot, which answered basic questions or directed users to a knowledge base. But once your need became complicated, perhaps with an exceptional circumstances refund request, an actual human took over. This is the real story: AI handles routine interactions, freeing up people to tackle work that needs judgment, empathy, or creative problem-solving. In banking, for example, algorithms scan thousands of transactions for fraud, flagging anything suspicious. Yet when a flagged case needs context or a nuanced explanation to a worried client, the job still falls to a person.

Another big misconception: "AI is always objective." In reality, AI systems reflect the data they're trained on, warts and all. Imagine a hiring tool that learns from past résumés. If those résumés carry hidden biases, the AI can end up favoring specific candidates over others. This isn't just theory; tech companies have pulled recruiting tools off the market after discovering these flaws. Data shapes outcomes, and sometimes data carries baggage from our very imperfect world. So, when you hear claims that AI makes "fair" or "unbiased" decisions, keep in mind it's only as neutral as its training material.

One more myth worth breaking is the idea that "AI can think." It's tempting to believe because chatbots can sound clever and image generators create art that rivals that of humans. However, what's happening is pattern-following, rather than thinking or understanding. AI doesn't reason or imagine; it reacts to input with what is statistically likely to fit, based on its training. For example, an AI might write decent marketing copy or summarize documents with impressive speed. Yet if you ask it to catch sarcasm, say, "Great job on missing that deadline!" the model often misses the joke entirely or responds with something offbeat. Commonsense reasoning still trips up these systems, and nuanced legal advice or ethical judgment remains firmly in human hands.

On the ground, practical AI shows up in ways you might already use without realizing it. Scheduling assistants can review your calendar and suggest meeting times based on everyone's availability, a significant time-saver for busy teams. Document summarizers scan lengthy reports and deliver concise digests, so you don't have to slog through every page. Banks deploy AI to spot fraud by monitoring account activity for unusual patterns, a sudden ATM withdrawal in two distant cities, minutes apart, trips the system. In customer service, chatbots answer basic questions at any hour, keeping wait times down and customers content.

Despite these advances, AI struggles with tasks that require genuine insight or nuance. It can't reliably interpret sarcasm or humor. Ask an AI to respond to a joke, and you'll often get a flat or awkward reply. Commonsense reasoning is another blind spot; machines may flag an expense report for buying a $2 coffee as suspicious because they lack context. Even when asked for legal advice, AI can sound convincing while delivering incomplete or downright risky answers.

To keep hype in check, I use a simple reality test when I see big AI claims in the news or on product labels:

Reality Check:

- Does the tool automate tasks or replace entire jobs?

- Is there evidence of bias in the data or outcomes?

- Can the system clearly explain its recommendations?

If any answer is fuzzy, ask for more proof before trusting the product or story.

Quick Checklist for Assessing AI Products:

- What real-world problem does it solve?

- Are humans still involved for tricky cases?

- Does the tool make decisions you can understand, or does it feel like a black box?

Keep this checklist handy next time you see an "AI-powered" headline or demo. Validation beats hype every single time.

The Limits of Today's AI, or, What It Can and Can't Do

When you examine how AI works on a day-to-day basis, some stark limitations become apparent. Machines, despite their proficiency with patterns and numbers, often overlook what matters most in human relationships: emotional intelligence and empathy. AI can read thousands of customer reviews in seconds, but it doesn't "feel" joy, frustration, or hope. Have you ever chatted with a support bot after a rough day? In that case, you know the difference: the responses sound polite but hollow, missing the warmth or subtle understanding a person brings. AI cannot relate to someone's anxiety over a medical bill or celebrate with you when you land a new job. Even the most advanced systems can't pick up on the unspoken cues we convey in every conversation, such as tone, pauses, facial expressions, or the sigh hidden between words. That's why chatbots don't replace therapists and why teachers are irreplaceable when students need encouragement or reassurance.

Ambiguous situations trip up AI in a way that surprises many people. While machines excel at clear, repetitive tasks, such as sorting emails and flagging suspicious transactions, they falter when things become fuzzy or new. AI translation offers a perfect example. Give it an idiom, "It's raining cats and dogs," and you might get a literal translation that's laughably wrong in another language. Slang, regional quirks, or rare words often leave AI systems confused, resulting in responses that make no sense to locals. In business, a system trained on last year's market data might flounder when sudden world events change everything overnight. Novelty throws a wrench into the works because AI only knows what it has seen before; it doesn't improvise like people do.

Another issue that makes people uneasy is the "black box" nature of many AI systems. Imagine trusting a calculator that never shows its work and provides answers with no explanation. That's how many AIs operate: they spit out recommendations or scores, but even experts can't always say why one outcome appeared instead of another. Regulators and users alike are concerned about this opacity, particularly in fields such as finance and healthcare, where decisions have real consequences. Efforts to make AI more transparent have gained momentum recently, with new tools aiming to "open the box" and reveal some of the logic behind each answer. But explainable AI is still in its early days, and complete clarity remains elusive.

Bias is another lurking danger, one that goes far beyond simple technical mistakes. When AI is trained on data from the real world, it often picks up human prejudices without anyone meaning for it to happen. Hiring algorithms have been caught reinforcing gender or racial bias, favoring specific names or backgrounds over others simply because past decisions (often flawed) shaped their training data. Facial recognition software has made headlines for misidentifying people of color at much higher rates than white faces, leading to wrongful accusations and lost opportunities. Credit scoring systems have sometimes penalized applicants based on patterns associated with zip codes or demographics, rather than their financial behavior. These failures aren't rare; they're well-documented, and they show why blind faith in "objective" AI is so risky.

Because of these risks and blind spots, human oversight isn't just helpful, it's vital. The most innovative organizations employ "human-in-the-loop" setups, where people review AI outputs before taking action, particularly in areas such as hiring, medical diagnoses, or loan approvals. If a résumé screener flags your application as a "pass," a real person should double-check before your dreams end up in a digital trash bin. When an AI suggests treatment options for a patient, doctors weigh those results against their expertise and intuition. For everyday users, the rule is simple: trust AI for speed and routine tasks, but pause and double-check when the stakes are high or when something feels off.

If you're using AI tools at work or home, always ask: "Would I trust this answer if it came from a person I barely know?" If not, seek a second opinion or consider seeking more context before taking action. Use AI as an assistant, not as the final judge, especially when fairness, empathy, or creativity are at stake.

Infographics for Grasping Neural Networks and Data Flow

Understanding how data moves through an AI system can feel like navigating a maze at first, but visuals make it surprisingly clear. Picture the process as water flowing through a series of pipes, each section performing a distinct function. Initially, **data collection, including** raw information such as photos, texts, or numbers, begins, pouring in from various sources. Maybe you're collecting hundreds of images of handwritten numbers for a school project, or your business is gathering sales records from last year. This raw stream isn't yet ready for use, so it proceeds to the **preprocessing** stage. Think of this like filtering out leaves and sticks from the water. Here, data gets cleaned up: blurry pictures are removed, missing details are filled in, and outliers are set aside. The cleaner the input, the smoother the flow ahead.

After prepping, the data enters **training**, where the magic starts. Imagine a series of color-coded pipes: red for inputs (like the pixel values of a handwritten "8"), blue for hidden processes (where patterns begin to take shape), and green for outputs (the predicted digit at the end). During training, the system tries to connect input to output by adjusting its internal "knobs" to minimize errors. It's like tuning an equalizer on a stereo to get the perfect sound. Once trained, the pipeline is ready for **prediction**: you feed in new examples, and out comes a result, ideally fast and accurate.

Zooming in on neural networks, the architecture resembles a subway map. Picture circles lined up in columns; each circle is a neuron, a small processor tuned to spot a specific pattern. The first column takes in the raw input, such as the brightness of each pixel in a picture of a number. Lines (arrows) connect these inputs to the next column, the hidden layer, where each neuron combines bits of information from several inputs. Some neurons might light up when they spot a curve, while others light up when they see a straight line. This "team of pattern spotters" passes their findings to the final column, which makes the call: Is that scribble a 6 or an 8? The network layers act as filters, each one refining the picture until a confident answer emerges.

Metaphors help here. Imagine water splitting off into branches as it flows, each branch represents a "decision tree," with choices splitting again and again as data moves along. Or think of each neuron as a security guard at a concert gate: one looks for hats, another checks ticket stubs, another scans for smiles. Only when all checks line up does someone get waved through as "approved." This way, even without math or code, you can visualize how information gets sliced, checked, and combined.

Having visuals on hand is like keeping a map in your back pocket; you won't get lost when new terms show up in articles or product demos. And whenever you're explaining AI to friends or coworkers, you can pull out reference sheets to make your point stick. Understanding how data flows and transforms inside AI systems isn't just for engineers; it's for anyone who wants to feel less mystified and more in control when using new tools every day.

Visuals aren't just pretty pictures; they anchor ideas. When you see how each piece fits together, even the most complicated technology starts to feel approachable. Keep infographics handy as you continue exploring AI's role in everyday life. With this foundation in place, you'll be able to spot patterns more quickly and make more informed choices about where AI fits best in your routine.

Chapter Two

AI in Daily Life for Personal Productivity and Wellbeing

AI as Your Calendar Concierge who Schedules, Reminds, and Manages Smart To-Do Lists

Have you ever experienced that overwhelming feeling when you realize you've forgotten a crucial task or appointment? It's a common scenario that can lead to unnecessary stress. This is where AI-powered scheduling tools come in. They're not just digital calendars; they're your assistants, ready to anticipate your needs, fill in the gaps, and ensure you're always on time, sometimes even before you remember what's on your plate. It's like having a hyper-organized friend quietly running interference for you, relieving you from the burden of remembering every detail.

Let's talk about how these assistants work with the calendars you already use. Suppose you're a *Google Calendar* devotee, an *Outlook* loyalist, or you swear by *Apple Calendar*. In that case, AI can weave right into your routine. Many of these services now use natural language processing, so you don't have to click through endless menus. You type or speak, "Lunch with Alex next Friday at noon" or "Remind me to call Mom every Sunday evening," and the app takes care of it. No fussing with drop-downs or clicking through dates, just plain talk, and the system translates your words into actual events. These tools even catch when you double-book yourself, pinging you to resolve conflicts before they turn into headaches. Some platforms, like Google's Assistant or Microsoft's Cortana, even let you schedule by voice while you're driving or cooking, so you can keep your hands free and your plans on track.

But scheduling is only part of the equation. Staying productive means managing your priorities effectively. This is where next-gen to-do apps shine. Tools like *Todoist* now offer AI-driven prioritization, analyzing your habits, deadlines, and long-term goals to suggest what needs to be tackled first. If you finish reports last minute, it'll nudge those tasks up your list earlier next time. Apps like *Motion and Notion* go even further: they observe how you work and automatically adjust your daily agenda. For instance, if you typically respond to emails in the morning and struggle with creative work after lunch, the app learns your rhythm and blocks time for deep focus when you're most alert. It's like having a personal assistant who understands your work style and tailors your schedule to suit you accordingly.

Automation is where these tools truly shine. You can set recurring events, such as weekly grocery runs or monthly budget reviews, or even reminders to water your plants, so nothing falls through the cracks. Meal planning apps can slot dinner prep into open windows between meetings. Fitness routines get scheduled based on your preferred days and energy levels. Suppose you're leading a team at work. In that case, AI can automatically distribute weekly report deadlines and sync them with everyone's calendars, eliminating the need for countless emails back and forth. The best part is how seamlessly these platforms sync across devices. Add a task on your laptop at work, check it off from your phone on the train home, or ask your smart speaker to read out your agenda while making breakfast. The days of 'I forgot my list at home' are over. Your schedule follows you everywhere, saving you time and making you more efficient.

Of course, all this convenience raises questions about privacy and control. After all, when an AI assistant manages your day-to-day life, it knows a lot about you, who you meet, when you travel, even how often you reschedule dentist appointments. That's why picking privacy-first apps is worth your attention. Look for platforms that clearly outline their data policies in plain English and allow you to decide what data gets stored or shared (see Forbes, 2024). Most reputable apps now offer granular permission settings, allowing you to restrict access to specific calendars or block integration with external services altogether. Regularly reviewing your activity logs is also smart, as it lets you see what the assistant tracks and catch anything that feels off.

Some calendar tools allow for 'incognito' events or private notes that don't sync across devices or get analyzed by AI at all. For instance, you can mark a personal day off as 'incognito' so it doesn't affect your work schedule, or you can add a private note about a surprise party that won't be seen by anyone else. If privacy is a non-negotiable for you, check which apps support local-only data storage, meaning that nothing leaves your device unless you explicitly allow it (Europarl, 2020). And if the idea of an app micromanaging your time gives you pause, remember: the best AI assistants offer easy opt-outs for any automated suggestions or reminders that start to feel invasive.

Calendar Tune-Up Checklist

- Review which apps have access to your primary calendar(s).

- Try scheduling an event using only natural language, such as "Dinner with Jamie next Thursday at 7 pm."

- Set up a recurring reminder for something low-stress (like watering plants) as a test drive.

- Explore the privacy settings: Can you limit data sharing? Is there a log of activities you can review?

- Experiment with a smart to-do app like *Todoist* or *Notion*, let it analyze your habits for a week, and see what suggestions come up.

When AI handles the grunt work of planning and prioritizing, you end up with more time to live your life and a lot less stress over what might have slipped through the cracks.

Email Triage and Smart Summarization with AI

If your email inbox feels like a bottomless pit, you're not alone. Email has a way of multiplying overnight, and before you know it, you're staring at dozens, sometimes hundreds, of unread messages. It's a recipe for stress, missed opportunities, and that sinking feeling when something important gets buried under a pile of newsletters and promotions. Luckily, AI can now tackle this mess for you, sorting through the chaos and bringing order where there was only digital clutter.

AI-powered tools like *Gmail's Smart Reply* and *Smart Compose* are a game-changer for anyone who dreads typing out endless responses. *Thoughtful Reply* scans the content of emails and instantly suggests short, context-aware replies, think "Sounds good!" or "Let's meet at 3 pm." *Smart Compose* takes things further by predicting entire sentences as you type, saving you time and mental energy. You'll notice that over time, as you accept or reject these suggestions, the system learns your tone and common phrases, subtly shaping itself to sound more like you. This isn't just about efficiency, it's about making your digital communication feel natural and less robotic.

Some folks crave even more control over their inboxes, and that's where advanced tools like *Superhuman* and *SaneBox* come in. *Super-*

human's AI-powered triage sorts messages by urgency, highlighting what needs your attention right now and pushing distractions to the background. *SaneBox*, on the other hand, analyzes your email habits and filters out less essential messages into folders you can review later (or never). Newsletters, social updates, and receipts get whisked away from your primary inbox, so you only see what's truly pressing. Both tools recognize patterns in your reading and replying habits. If you always open emails from your boss but ignore weekly sales pitches, the algorithm learns to make those distinctions for you.

Getting started with AI-powered filters is surprisingly straightforward. In *Gmail*, head to Settings and find the "Filters and Blocked Addresses" section. Here, you can create rules for newsletters, bills, or anything else that clogs up your inbox. Perhaps you would like all bank statements to be stored in a "Finance" folder or unsubscribe links to be flagged for easy removal. *Superhuman* asks you to mark emails as "important" or "skip," then builds tailored rules behind the scenes. *SaneBox* works by dragging messages into custom folders, such as "SaneLater" or "SaneBlackHole." The latter is ideal for senders you never want to hear from again. For newsletters you'd rather not receive, AI-powered unsubscribe services can scan your inbox and identify recurring senders, allowing you to review and remove them with one click. This eliminates the hassle of searching for unsubscribe links that are often buried at the bottom of emails.

Automation is powerful, but it shouldn't run unchecked. There are moments when you'll want to keep a human eye on things, especially with sensitive or confidential emails. Most platforms allow you to flag specific senders or keywords (such as "confidential," "urgent," or even your boss's name) so that those messages always land in your primary inbox for manual review. It's a safety net that ensures nothing slips through that matters. For everyday replies, trust the AI to handle routine requests, meeting confirmations, or generic follow-ups. When a message requires nuance, such as negotiating a contract or responding to a complaint from a major client, it's better to pause and craft your response. Remember that while AI gets tone right most of the time, it can stumble with sarcasm or subtle cues.

Accessibility is an area where AI email tools shine for busy folks and neurodiverse users alike. Many platforms now support voice-activated email management. You can ask *Google Assistant* or *Siri* to read key messages aloud while you're on the go or multitasking at home. For individuals who struggle with reading lengthy emails or processing large amounts of information simultaneously, daily summary digests are a lifesaver. These tools scan your inbox at set times, bundle everything necessary into a single summary, and deliver it first thing in the morning or whenever you choose. You don't have to scroll endlessly; review one digest, then decide what needs your attention.

Suppose you're someone who likes to keep their hands free or who finds traditional email interfaces overwhelming. In that case, voice assistants can draft replies as you dictate or even archive messages with simple commands. Some platforms also offer distraction-free modes, showing only urgent emails until you're ready to dive into the rest. For those who need extra help staying organized, AI can flag action items within messages ("Please send the report by Friday") and add them directly to your task app or calendar.

A few tips can go a long way in staying balanced: let AI handle repetitive tasks and routine responses, but check in on essential threads before sending anything sensitive. Customize your filters so that nothing critical is missed, but let automation handle the heavy lifting for everything else. Over time, you'll notice less stress, more time back in your day, and an inbox that finally feels under control, without sacrificing security or your personal touch.

Use AI as Your Personal Research Assistant for Finding and Organizing Information

Browsing the web for answers can feel like wandering through a maze of ads, pop-ups, and questionable sources. AI search assistants are changing that game. Now, instead of sifting through dozens of links, you can use tools like *Perplexity* AI to chat and get the info you need in plain language. Think of it like texting a brainy friend who happens to have a vast digital library at their fingertips. You type in your question, "What's the difference between oat milk and almond milk?" or "Summarize the main ideas from this 10-page PDF," and *Perplexity* responds with clear, concise answers, often with links to sources so you can double-check facts for yourself. The magic here isn't just speed; it's relevance. Conversational AI search engines cut through clutter and point you straight to what matters, instead of sending you down endless rabbit holes.

Sometimes you're staring at a monstrous article or a research report so dense it could double as a doorstop. Instead of slogging through every paragraph, you can copy the text into *ChatGPT* or a similar AI writing tool. These assistants scan the content and generate a summary in seconds, so you get the highlights, no headache required. It's not just about trimming fat; it's about ensuring you capture the big ideas without missing anything critical. Whether you're prepping for a meeting or just trying to stay informed, this approach saves serious time.

Organizing what you find can be another battle. Bookmarks pile up, notes scatter across apps, and before long, you're not sure where anything lives. This is where AI-powered note and knowledge management steps in. *Notion's* AI features can now automatically sort your notes by topic. Imagine you're planning a vacation. One note is about hotels, another about sights to see, and a third includes your flight numbers. *Notion* detects the themes and sorts them into neat categories. If you're working on a group project or studying for an exam, all related materials for a single subject are grouped. *Mem* AI takes this even further by watching what you save and building a knowledge base behind the scenes. You drop in articles, snippets, or even voice notes; *Mem* connects the dots using AI, linking related topics so that when you search later, all your best info pops up together.

Students will recognize the struggle of wrangling sources for essays and research projects. AI is a game-changer here. Instead of flipping between endless journal databases, AI research assistants scrape trusted academic sources, pull up relevant papers, and even help format citations in APA or MLA style. Need a quick literature review? Feed your topic into an AI assistant, and it generates a summary along with links to foundational studies. For grad students staring down a mountain of reading, this means less time searching and more time understanding the material.

Professionals also benefit from these tools; competitive research that once took days now happens in hours. Suppose you need to know how your company stacks up against the competition or what the latest trends are in your industry. AI search bots scan market reports, news articles, and even social media chatter to provide a digestible overview. The same applies to sales teams tracking leads or HR departments seeking to benchmark salaries; AI identifies and compiles key details without requiring endless manual effort.

Lifelong learners and hobbyists are also included. You'd like to teach yourself photography or explore urban gardening. AI-curated reading lists are here for that. Just type your interest into a tool like *Mem* or *Notion's* AI engine. It generates a list of recommended articles, videos, and forums, often ranked by trustworthiness or popularity, so you know where to start. This eliminates a lot of guesswork from self-education, making it easier to pursue new passions without feeling overwhelmed.

With all this convenience comes responsibility; AI can sometimes "hallucinate" facts or pull outdated info from shady corners of the internet. That's why it's smart to make critical thinking part of your routine. Always verify essential details with the sources whenever possible. If an AI says something surprising or suspicious, scan the links it provides and verify if they are accurate on official websites or reputable publications. Many tools allow you to set up alerts for fact-checking, which notify you when reputable fact-checkers or news organizations have flagged claims in your reading.

Quick Fact-Check

Copy a summary provided by any AI assistant about a current event or scientific finding. Pick two claims that seem important or surprising. Search for those claims on official news websites or academic databases to see if they match. Note where the AI got things right, and where it missed or exaggerated.

Using AI as your personal research assistant isn't about taking shortcuts; it's about working smarter and keeping your learning organized, without getting bogged down in details or distractions.

Using AI to Shop Smarter for Product Comparisons and Price Tracking

Shopping has gotten a lot smarter, and it's not just because stores have fancy apps. These days, AI-powered tools do the heavy lifting, turning what used to be a weekend project of scouring reviews and hunting for deals into a streamlined, stress-free experience. When you start looking for a new gadget, such as a pair of headphones or a kitchen blender, AI comparison engines scan thousands of reviews, product features, and prices in seconds. For instance, *Google Shopping* now utilizes machine learning to suggest products tailored to your needs, weighing specifications, ratings, and even user questions to help you identify the best fit. It's not just about picking the item with the highest score; the AI takes into account what matters to people like you, whether that's quiet motors in a vacuum cleaner or battery life in wireless earbuds.

Fake reviews have become a real headache, especially on those end-less product pages with suspiciously glowing five-star ratings. This is where *Fakespot* comes in handy. It runs each review through an algorithm that flags patterns typical of bots and paid shills, helping you separate genuine feedback from the fluff. You receive a letter grade indicating the trustworthiness of the reviews, a quick reality check before you make a purchase. Beyond that, browser extensions like *Honey* run in the background. At the same time, you shop online, automatically searching for coupons and applying them at checkout. No more copying endless codes from shady websites; *Honey's* AI sifts through what works, so you don't waste time on expired or fake deals.

Finding the lowest price used to mean flipping between multiple store tabs, waiting for sales, or signing up for a dozen email lists that clog your inbox. Now, AI tools let you set up price alerts that monitor deals for you. Sites like *CamelCamelCamel* track *Amazon* prices over time. You pick an item, set your target price, and when the cost drops, you receive an alert, as simple as that. It even shows historical trends, so you can determine if today's "deal" is truly a bargain or just a marketing ploy. For shoppers who bounce between retailers, *Price.com* compares offers from dozens of stores at once, highlighting not just discounts but also shipping costs and return policies. This way, you don't get tripped up by a deal that looks good on the surface but costs more once you factor in hidden fees.

Scams and counterfeit goods are everywhere these days. AI-driven browser add-ons can identify suspicious sellers by analyzing their history, such as sudden spikes in negative feedback or mismatched contact information. When an offer seems too good to be true, these tools put up a warning banner or even block access until you confirm it's safe. Automated systems now report suspicious deals directly to the platform or even to consumer protection agencies if they identify enough red flags. That extra layer of digital street smarts can be the difference between snagging a sweet deal and getting burned by a fake.

Ethical shopping is becoming easier with the help of AI. You may prefer shoes made without animal products or tech gadgets from companies with robust labor standards. Some browser plugins and shopping sites now rate brands for sustainability based on third-party certifications and public records. They gather data on fair wages, carbon footprints, cruelty-free guarantees, and more, then score or label products accordingly. You can filter results to show only eco-friendly or locally made items at the top of your feed. If you care about supporting small businesses or minimizing your environmental impact, these tools make it practical instead of overwhelming.

For example, if you're buying coffee beans and want something fair-trade certified, tick a filter and watch as mainstream brands drop off your list. At the same time, ethical options emerge as the top choice. AI even helps spot greenwashing, when brands exaggerate their eco credentials by comparing claims to real certifications and watchdog reports. Some apps send notifications when a new sustainable brand enters the market or when your favorite product gets a higher ethical rating after changing suppliers.

There's also peace of mind knowing that these systems respect your privacy more than most people expect. Most tools only analyze shopping data locally on your device or use anonymized info to find better deals without tracking your identity everywhere you go. Many allow you to clear your history with a single click or select which sites you can access.

The whole experience feels like having an extremely meticulous friend whose only hobby is finding bargains and being vigilant against scams. You get better prices and smarter picks while also knowing if that "eco-friendly" label means something tangible. As these AI shopping assistants keep improving, shopping becomes less about stress and more about confidence, both that you got the best deal and that your purchase matches your values.

AI-Powered Health for Fitness Coaching to Mental Wellness Apps

Getting in shape or finding some mental breathing room used to mean hiring a personal trainer, joining a gym, or squeezing in an appointment with a counselor between work and dinner. Now, AI steps into that coaching role. Sometimes better than any clipboard-toting fitness guru could. AI-powered fitness apps have revolutionized the way we approach movement and health. Instead of static workout plans, you receive a routine that adapts and evolves in tandem with your habits and goals. The *Freeletics* AI coach, for example, analyzes your feedback after every session. Did that workout leave you wiped out or wanting more? The app tweaks tomorrow's plan, factoring in your soreness, sleep, and even the time you have available. *Fitbit* takes things further with activity insights. It tracks steps, heart rate, and sleep, then serves up suggestions tailored to your actual patterns, maybe nudging you to reach a new goal or reminding you when you've been too sedentary. *Peloton's* adaptive routines recognize when you need a push or a break; if you skip a class, it adjusts your schedule so you're not playing catch-up or feeling guilty.

The impact goes beyond numbers and stats. These apps are designed to send timely reminders, celebrate milestones, and sometimes gamify progress, making it feel like you're leveling up in real life. No more wondering if you should repeat that same HIIT circuit for the tenth time; AI sorts through endless possibilities and picks what works for you today, not just what's trending. Suppose you've got an injury or special need. In that case, the more innovative apps quickly adapt, not just swapping out exercises, but actively learning which moves to avoid and which help you progress safely. This sort of personalization would be impossible with a paper plan or static video playlist.

Physical health is only half the picture these days. Stress, anxiety, and the general noise of modern life mean more people are reaching for digital solutions to boost mental wellbeing. AI is there too, quietly offering support without judgment or a waiting room. The *Wysa* AI chatbot is one example; it's like texting with a supportive friend who knows all the best coping strategies. You type about your rough day or your mood swings, and *Wysa* responds with evidence-based advice, guided exercises, or simply a space to vent. *Woebot* is similar, but it leans more heavily into cognitive behavioral therapy techniques. It helps you spot negative thinking patterns and gently guides you toward reframing those thoughts with interactive conversation. No awkward silences, no fear of "bothering" someone, you get feedback right when you need it.

Calm, one of the most popular mindfulness apps, utilizes AI to suggest meditation tracks tailored to your stress levels or recent activity. Maybe you've had a string of restless nights; *Calm* picks up on that and nudges you toward sleep stories or breathing exercises designed to quiet your mind. These tools don't replace therapists or doctors. Still, they fill a gap, especially when you need relief outside traditional office hours.

There's a line where AI in health is a great coach, and where it simply can't (and shouldn't) take the wheel. It's easy to get comfortable relying on chatbots for tough days or letting an app take control of your exercise plan. However, red flags appear when an app claims to diagnose complex conditions or aggressively promotes in-app purchases tied to "miracle" results. If your symptoms are severe, unexplained pain, deep depression, or panic attacks, licensed human professionals must step in. No algorithm can replace decades of experience or offer the empathy needed in crisis moments.

Another risk arises from sharing sensitive details with digital platforms that may not always prioritize your interests. Before trusting any health app, please take a close look at its privacy promises. Reputable platforms use end-to-end encryption, meaning your data is scrambled so that not even the app provider can access it. Dive into those data-sharing policies. Do they sell anonymized stats to advertisers? Can you export or delete your info with one click? If not, that's a warning sign. Regularly review app permissions on your phone; if an app requests access to contacts or the microphone without a clear connection to your health goals, consider limiting or revoking those permissions.

Opt for apps that give you control, clear dashboards that show what's being tracked, and let you pause data collection whenever you want. It's also smart to check whether the company is transparent about security breaches and regularly updates its software. Your health journey should be private unless you choose otherwise.

Digital wellness isn't about letting robots run your life; it's about harnessing today's advances to provide real support that fits seamlessly into your busy world. When you use these tools wisely, knowing when to lean in and when to reach out for human help, you end up with more energy, more precise focus, and peace of mind.

This chapter demonstrates how AI can transform daily routines, from exercising and calming the mind to safeguarding private health data. As technology becomes more ingrained in our lives, understanding where it fits and where it doesn't is what gives us real power. In the next chapter, we'll explore how these same tools can help families and educators create balance, support learning, and make life at home run more smoothly for everyone.

Chapter Three

AI for Families, Parents, and Educators

AI Tools for Student Tutoring and Study Skills

Your kids are sitting at the dining table in the evening, working on open laptops and half-completed worksheets. You're stirring pasta, fielding math questions, and fighting the urge to Google every homework problem under the sun. If that sounds familiar, you're not alone. So many families wrestle with the homework crunch, especially when teachers send home work that feels light years beyond what you remember from your school days. Here's where AI-powered homework helpers step in, not to replace you or even your child's teacher, but to make the whole process feel less like a battle and more like a team effort.

Innovative tutoring platforms are making a big difference for families. Take *Khan Academy's AI tutor*: it doesn't just spit out answers. It leads students through math or science problems one logical step at a time, pausing to check for understanding before moving on. If your child stumbles, the AI breaks the problem down further, serving up hints or similar practice questions until the concept clicks. The tone is patient and never judgmental, something that can be a breath of fresh air after a long day. And it's not just math; science concepts from photosynthesis to Newton's laws get that same supportive treatment.

Then there's *Socratic by Google*, which turns any phone into an instant homework sidekick. Your student snaps a photo of a tricky question, anything from algebra to English literature, and *Socratic* scans its massive database for clear explanations. It highlights relevant concepts, links to concise lessons, and even offers brief videos that break down complex ideas into manageable pieces. The brilliance here is how it meets kids where they are: no more digging through dense textbooks or scrolling endless forums. Help arrives in seconds, tailored to the exact question at hand. This not only saves time but also makes the learning process more efficient, reducing stress for both parents and students.

If you want to move beyond "just get it done," AI study aids offer personalized ways to build skills over time. *Quizlet's* AI-generated flashcards take the old-school index card method and supercharge it. Your learner can create their own study sets or tap into millions made by other students and teachers. The AI analyzes their answers, identifies weak spots, and reshuffles cards to ensure that more rigid material receives more attention. It even creates short quizzes and games, turning review time into something a little more engaging, maybe even fun on a good day.

Language learning gets an upgrade with apps like *Duolingo*. The app's AI reviews each user's mistakes and progress, then adjusts future exercises so that challenging words or grammar rules pop up more frequently. No two learners get precisely the same practice. If your teen breezes through verb conjugations but struggles with vocabulary, *Duolingo* automatically shifts its focus. You'll notice how it encourages streaks and daily practice by celebrating milestones and gently nudging when motivation starts to fade.

Of course, technology can never fully replace the care of a caring adult or the guidance of a skilled teacher. It's tempting to let AI "do the work." Still, real learning sticks best when students actively engage with explanations and reflect on mistakes. I always encourage families to treat these tools as supplements, not shortcuts. After using *Khan Academy* or *Socratic*, ask your student to explain the solution in their own words. If something sounds off or too easy, have them double-check with a textbook or ask their teacher for clarification. Parental review is still key; occasionally, sit in on an AI-powered homework session or scan through the explanations together. These tools are not just aids; they are empowering resources that can help students build confidence and independence in their learning, one problem at a time.

To make these platforms truly useful (and not just another distraction), try weaving them into your family's routine. Perhaps you set aside 30 minutes after dinner as a "homework power hour," where everyone brings their most challenging questions to the table and works alongside their chosen AI helper. Some families find it helpful to create a shared calendar event for "study time," so phones and laptops get used for learning instead of scrolling social media. AI-generated study planners can help organize assignments, prioritize tasks by deadline or difficulty, and even break big projects into bite-sized steps spread over several days.

Family Study Session Checklist

- Pick one AI homework tool (like *Khan Academy* or *Socratic*) and walk through a problem together.

- Please have your student explain what they learned to you; teach-back is powerful reinforcement.

- Set up *Quizlet* flashcards for an upcoming quiz and review them together in game mode.

- Schedule a regular "tech break" where your child practices explaining concepts without any digital help.

- Reflect at the end of the week: What worked? What felt confusing? Adjust tools or routines as needed.

Hovering over every assignment isn't needed, but showing kids how to use these resources wisely helps them build independence and confidence, one problem at a time.

AI for Digital Safety and Content Filtering for Parental Peace of Mind

Keeping your kids safe online can often feel like a never-ending game of catch-up. New apps appear, trends spread overnight, and suddenly your child's phone is buzzing with notifications from corners of the internet you've never heard of. It's exhausting to monitor everything by hand. That's where AI-powered parental control tools step up, acting as invisible sentinels that watch for trouble without breathing down your child's neck all day. Apps like *Bark* use machine learning to scan messages, social media posts, and even photos for early signs of cyberbullying, explicit content, or conversations with strangers. Instead of reading every text yourself, you get alerts only when something risky pops up. *Bark's* algorithm doesn't just look for banned words; it understands context, so if your child is joking with friends or genuinely upset, you'll know the difference. This goes beyond simple keyword blocking; it's about recognizing patterns that might signal a real problem before it spirals out of control, providing you with a sense of relief and peace of mind.

Qustodio brings another layer of security with its smart web filters. It automatically blocks dangerous or inappropriate sites and can even restrict access to specific categories, such as gambling or violent games, without requiring you to toggle endless switches. The system adapts based on what your child tries to visit, learning over time which sites are safe in your house and which aren't. You don't need to be a tech expert to set it up, pick the filters that match your family's values, and let *Qustodio* handle the rest. The app provides a clear dashboard showing what your kids are viewing and when they're active online. Suppose you notice something unusual, such as a spike in late-night browsing or repeated attempts to access blocked content. In that case, you can intervene and have a conversation before a bad habit takes hold.

Screen time is another battleground in most homes. It's easy for hours to slip away on *YouTube* or *Roblox*, especially after homework is done and dinner is over. AI-driven dashboards enable you to set daily limits without drama or constant reminders. For instance, you can automate device "bedtimes" so that all connected gadgets go dark automatically at 9 p.m. No more wrestling tablets out of hands when it's lights out. These tools generate daily usage reports, summarizing not just total hours, but also where that time was spent: on games, social media, reading, or chatting. Some apps break down usage by app or website, highlighting any new trends so you can spot potential problems early on. If your child suddenly spends an hour a night on an unfamiliar platform, you'll see the spike and can check it out together.

With all this monitoring power comes a fundamental responsibility: protecting your child's privacy as much as their safety. Not every app deserves access to your family's data. Look for tools with transparent privacy policies, no hidden fine print, or sneaky data sales to advertisers. The best platforms enable you to control what gets collected and where it goes, providing options to delete old logs or restrict sharing altogether. As kids grow older and start seeking more independence, these settings become even more crucial. You might dial back monitoring for a responsible high schooler while keeping tighter controls for younger siblings. Many apps now offer adjustable levels for different age groups, allowing you to loosen boundaries as trust builds gradually.

It's tempting to hope that technology alone can solve every online risk. But AI-powered filters have their flaws—sometimes flagging innocent chats as dangerous (false positives) or missing subtler dangers hidden in memes and slang (false negatives). No system is perfect; teenagers are especially crafty at finding ways around restrictions if they're determined enough. That's why no digital tool replaces open conversation. It pays to sit down regularly with your kids and explain not just what's blocked, but why those boundaries exist. Ask them what apps their friends use, what trends they're seeing, and how they feel about the restrictions in place. Ensure they know how to identify scams, avoid sharing personal information, and reach out if something online makes them uncomfortable.

Digital Safety Family Contract

Print out or write a short agreement as a family. List which apps are allowed, what screen time limits exist, and how alerts will be handled—will you talk first before taking action? Include spaces for everyone (including parents) to sign, then post it near the family computer or charging station.

No AI tool will ever replace your judgment as a parent. Still, the right combination of smart filters, clear boundaries, and honest dialogue can make the digital landscape feel less like a minefield and more like a place where your kids can explore safely and confidently every day.

Personalized Support Without Coding Using AI for Neurodiverse Learners

Suppose you've ever watched a neurodiverse student wrestle with reading, writing, or staying focused. In that case, you know how challenging and isolating schoolwork can feel. No two learners are the same, especially for those with ADHD, dyslexia, or autism. The proper support isn't always available in the classroom. As a parent or educator, it's easy to feel helpless or stretched thin. What has changed in the last couple of years is the extent to which AI can offer, not as a replacement for human care, but as a true partner in individualized learning. These tools don't need you to code, configure, or spend hours troubleshooting. They work in the background, adjusting to the student's pace and needs.

Take reading, for example. A lot of kids with dyslexia or ADHD find dense text overwhelming. *Speechify* is a lifesaver here—it turns any written material into spoken words, instantly. You can snap a photo of textbook pages or upload assignments, and *Speechify* reads them aloud in clear, natural voices. Students can listen on the bus, at home, or while doodling—whatever helps them process information best. The speed is adjustable; someone who wants to slow down tricky passages can do so, while another student might prefer a brisk read-through to keep their mind from wandering. For writing struggles, *Ghotit* steps in. This tool was built specifically with dyslexic students in mind.

It checks spelling and grammar but goes further by catching "real word" mistakes, like mixing up "their," "there," and "they're," and offering context-sensitive suggestions. *Ghotit's* interface is clean and distraction-free, so kids can focus on ideas instead of getting tripped up by mechanics.

Multi-sensory engagement is where many neurodiverse students shine. Some individuals thrive on visuals, while others require hearing information or interacting physically with content. *Otter.ai* is a powerful ally for students who process spoken words better than written ones. During lessons or group projects, *Otter* records speech and creates real-time transcripts. Learners can review what was said, highlight key points, or replay important explanations at their own pace. It's beneficial when note-taking is difficult or attention drifts. For daily structure, *Time Timer* offers visual schedules that break the day into clear blocks—morning routine, homework, break time—using colors and simple icons. This helps reduce anxiety about what comes next and makes transitions smoother for kids who struggle with changes in routine.

Accessibility features have also evolved significantly. Built-in reading modes strip away clutter from digital pages, eliminating flashing ads and distracting sidebars, leaving just the core text in an easy-to-read format. Some apps allow you to customize screen layouts to enhance comfort, such as changing background colors for improved contrast, increasing font size, or adding spacing between lines. Predictive text tools anticipate what the student might want to write next, reducing typing time and frustration. Voice commands enable students to ask questions or navigate apps hands-free, great for those who find keyboards challenging or want to minimize distractions.

For focus, many devices now offer modes that block pop-ups and silence notifications during study sessions. Students work in a digital "quiet zone," making it easier to focus on tasks without constant interruptions. These minor tweaks add up; suddenly, learning feels less like an uphill battle and more like an achievable challenge.

As a parent or teacher, you don't need a tech degree to find or use these tools. Most offer free trials, allowing you to test them with your child before making a commitment. Additionally, numerous user reviews break down the strengths and quirks of different products for various needs. Start by matching features to your student's unique goals: does your child need help decoding text? Go for text-to-speech tools like *Speechify*. Struggling with writing? Try *Ghotit's* error correction and feedback. Looking for real-time audio support? *Otter.ai's* transcription might be the ticket.

It helps to check app stores for accessibility ratings and look for endorsements from organizations focused on neurodiversity. Many platforms align their features with common Individualized Education Plan (IEP) objectives, such as improved reading accuracy, better organization, or stronger written expression, allowing you to track real progress over time. Don't be afraid to switch things up if something doesn't click; what works for one student may not for another, even within the same diagnosis.

Top AI Tools for Neurodiverse Learners

- *Speechify* (text-to-speech reading)

- *Ghotit* (dyslexia-friendly writing help)

- *Otter.ai* (audio transcription and note-taking)

- *Time Timer* (visual scheduling)

- Built-in device accessibility options (focus modes, custom layouts)

Experiment with these options one at a time, and ask your child what feels helpful or frustrating as you go along. Lean into their feedback, and adjust settings until you find a rhythm that works. The proper AI support can mean less stress at homework time, more independence for your learner, and fewer battles over getting things done. For educators, these tools open doors for inclusion in the classroom without adding hours of extra prep; it's about supporting every student's path to success with technology that adapts, not the other way around.

Creative Projects at Home using AI for Art, Music, and Storytelling

Family time can feel a bit stale when everyone's glued to their screen or the weather keeps you inside. Suppose you're looking to shake things up and make something memorable together. In that case, AI-powered creative tools are a wild card that can turn "just another night in" into something surprisingly cool. You don't need to be an artist, a musician, or even particularly techy. With just a few clicks or taps, you and your kids can co-create digital artwork, compose catchy tunes, or spin up wild stories—sometimes all in the same evening.

Let's start with visual art. Tools like *DALL-E* and *Craiyon* let you type in a phrase ("a cat riding a skateboard in the rain" or "a castle made of candy") and instantly see vivid images pop up on your screen. It's like having a digital paintbrush that never runs out of new ideas. Kids can guide the process, tweaking prompts or combining wacky concepts to see what emerges. Sometimes the results are beautiful; other times, they're hilariously weird. Either way, it sparks laughter and conversation. These images can serve as the starting point for larger projects: print them and create your storybooks, use them as backdrops for school presentations, or even turn them into custom greeting cards for friends and family.

Music gets a similar AI twist. *Chrome Music Lab* is my go-to for hands-on family music nights. Its *Song Maker* experiment lets anyone, whether a serious musician or a total beginner, lay down melodies by clicking colorful blocks on a grid. You hear instant feedback, so there's no guessing about what works. Kids can experiment with rhythm, layer sounds from different instruments, and watch how simple changes make the whole song feel different. This tool is a lifesaver for school projects about sound or rhythm, but it's also just plain fun. Try challenging each other to create the weirdest melody or recreate favorite TV theme songs from memory. Because everything happens in the browser, setting up takes seconds, and there's no need to install anything or read complicated instructions.

Storytelling gets a turbo boost with AI chatbots like *ChatGPT*. Gather everyone around, throw out a story prompt ("Write about a dragon who hates fire" or "Describe a picnic on Mars"), and watch as the AI drafts the beginnings of a tale you can all build on together. Each person can add a twist, a new character, or change the ending as you go. It's collaborative creativity at its best, no one needs to be "the writer" because everyone has input, and the AI keeps things moving if you ever get stuck for ideas. Sometimes, these stories become family inside jokes or are turned into short plays for rainy-day performances.

How does this all fit into learning? Projects like these feed the imagination and foster teamwork, while also incorporating lessons about digital tools and creative thinking. When kids use AI for artwork or music, it's a chance to talk about what makes something original. Is an image truly "yours" if a program helped create it? Most AI art and music tools let you download or share your creations, but some have restrictions or ask you to credit the AI platform. It's smart to check usage rights on each tool. Some images are free for personal use but not for commercial purposes, such as selling T-shirts or publishing in books. This is a great entry point for explaining the basics of copyright: respecting artists' work, avoiding plagiarism by not claiming someone else's creation as your own, and understanding the concept of fair use.

Encouraging respect for creators goes beyond legality. Teach kids to consider where inspiration comes from; many AI models are trained on thousands of existing songs, photos, and stories scraped from the web. If your child wants to put their AI-generated art online or use it in class assignments, have a quick chat about giving credit where it's due and not copying others' work outright. Some families make digital portfolios, a private collection of everyone's favorite pieces, stored on a shared drive or printed in photo books for family viewing. This keeps things meaningful (and safe) without the pressure of sharing every doodle with the world.

Before letting kids post AI creations publicly, please take a few minutes to review what they've made together. Is the image or story appropriate? Does it reveal any private info? Setting some ground rules for safe sharing, such as using first names only, avoiding personal photos, and thinking twice before posting anything that could embarrass someone later, keeps creative exploration positive for everyone.

For families who love structure, try themed creative nights: one week could be "AI Art Gallery" night where everyone generates and presents their exhibition; another could be "Robot Band Practice," creating group songs in *Chrome Music Lab*; next time, maybe "Spin-A-Story," where *ChatGPT* helps start tales that you finish aloud together around the dinner table. Mix things up by using images as story prompts or adding music to your narratives.

The point isn't perfection, it's about laughing together, discovering new interests, and showing kids (and yourself) that technology can be a tool for joy and self-expression rather than just another distraction. When everyone is involved, these little experiments become shared memories that outlast any single masterpiece.

Building Digital Literacy by Teaching Kids to Use AI Responsibly

Digital literacy goes beyond just using devices or apps. Especially with AI, it means understanding how these systems "think," make decisions, and sometimes make mistakes no human would. Most kids already use AI daily. Through voice assistants, chatbots, or even photo filters, often without realizing it. True digital literacy means questioning and thinking critically about what happens behind the scenes. Kids should understand that AI lacks feelings, intentions, and common sense. Its predictions are based on pattern detection in data, which means it can easily make bizarre mistakes, such as translating a phrase inaccurately or mistaking a dog for a muffin in a photo. Explaining this helps kids see AI as only a tool—one that isn't magical or guaranteed to be accurate.

Media literacy is crucial, too. Deepfake videos and audio clips are becoming increasingly convincing each year, making it increasingly difficult to distinguish between real and fake content. Kids are especially vulnerable in a culture where "seeing is believing" no longer holds. Teach them to spot deepfake warning signs, like odd eye movements, mismatched lips, or robotic speech. Show how AI can generate fake news, voice clones, or edited photos with little effort. Stress that anyone, including adults, can be fooled, but that the best defense is curiosity and caution: double-checking sources, favoring reputable outlets, and asking trusted adults for help.

Talks about AI don't have to be lectures. Use age-appropriate conversations. For younger children, keep it basic: "*Alexa* doesn't understand, it's just guessing using your words." Make family rules, such as not sharing personal information with voice assistants. For older kids, try role-play: "If *Siri* gave you medical advice, would you believe it? Why or why not?" Let them debate and become comfortable questioning, rather than unquestioningly trusting, technology. These habits promote healthy skepticism as they use more advanced AI.

Hands-on exploration helps kids understand AI's strengths and weaknesses. Encourage them to experiment with chatbots, not just for fun, but to test where the tech works and fails. They can use AI for conversation practice, pose silly riddles, or see how it reacts to unexpected prompts. Older kids might enjoy basic "If-This-Then-That" automations, which allow them to link actions between different apps. These activities reinforce logic and will enable them to glimpse how AI decision trees work, all without needing to code.

Curiosity flourishes when parents and teachers model it as well. If your child asks how a phone recognizes faces, turn it into a joint research project. Look up simple explanations or find kid-friendly videos together that clarify how AI detects patterns. Encourage questions like: "How does this work?" "Why did the bot answer that way?" "Could this tool be tricked?" Discuss real-life AI slip-ups, such as an assistant texting the wrong contact or a recommendation algorithm suggesting an unsuitable video. Treat these errors as learning moments rather than failures.

Empathy matters in digital spaces. Remind kids that there are real people behind most online identities, even if avatars or usernames seem fake. When using AI features in games or social apps, emphasize kindness and respect, as someone is always on the other side (or might become tomorrow's creator). Praise responsible use, like practicing language with chatbots instead of copying homework, or building automations that help the family stay organized.

Digital literacy isn't a one-time lesson; it evolves with technology. Stay curious together, keep learning, and don't hesitate to admit when you don't know something. Often, the best discoveries come from figuring things out as a family.

Family "AI Detective" Game

During meals or downtime, pick a viral video or meme that seems overly polished. Ask everyone: Was this made by a human or AI? What clues gave it away? Who can spot the most hints of editing or fakery? Celebrate creative thinking, not just correct answers.

In summary, digital literacy prepares your family to navigate technology with confidence. With curiosity, caution, and creativity, AI becomes less mysterious and more empowering. Next, we'll explore how professionals can apply these same skills and tools at work to achieve greater impact and reduce stress.

Chapter Four

AI for Business

Automating the Mundane Using AI for Scheduling, Note-Taking, and Meeting Recaps

Imagine the relief when you see an AI assistant effortlessly organizing a chaotic week of meetings. No more constant email ping-pong, just a silent AI scheduler in the background, finding time slots, checking time zones, and sending reminders to all participants. It's like hiring a hyper-efficient assistant without incurring additional payroll costs, offering immediate relief and a boost in productivity.

Here's how this plays out: Tools like *x.ai* and *Clara* operate as digital secretaries. When you copy them into a chat or email thread ("Hey Clara, please schedule something for next week"), they handle the back-and-forth, compare calendars, and suggest slots that match everyone's availability. They never sleep, so if someone responds at 2 a.m., the AI keeps things moving. For global or distributed teams, this avoids the headache of time zone conversions. If someone cancels or requests a reschedule, the AI handles it instantly, saving you from having to send awkward or repetitive coordination messages.

AI-powered notetakers, such as *Otter.ai* and *Fireflies*, join your *Zoom* or *Teams* meetings (with your consent) and transcribe conversations in real-time. They recognize and highlight key moments, like 'Let's revisit this' or 'I'll handle the report' flagging decisions and tasks. This not only saves you from the tedious task of taking notes but also ensures you never miss a crucial detail, allowing you to focus on the discussion at hand.

These tools go further than transcribing. *Otter.ai*, for example, creates recaps with major topics, tasks, and deadlines in plain English. *Fireflies* not only summarizes but also lets you assign tasks within the notes, so everyone knows their next steps, eliminating the need to dig through endless email threads. Since notes are digital, you can search by project, date, or keywords to monitor progress over weeks and months without sorting through piles of documents.

Integrating AI tools into your existing workflow is simpler than you think. Most AI scheduling and note-taking tools provide seamless integrations with popular platforms, including *Zoom*, *Teams*, and *Slack*. This means you can connect a meeting bot to a *Slack* channel, where highlights and recaps are automatically shared with the team. *Teams*-compatible bots can send summaries to group feeds or trigger reminders before deadlines. These tools often sync everything, bridging gaps between tools and ensuring that everyone is on the same page.

While AI tools offer convenience, it's crucial to consider privacy and accuracy. Always ensure that all participants are aware and give their consent before using AI notetakers. Most apps alert users when recording starts, but it's best practice to share this information up-front. For sensitive meetings, such as those involving HR issues, consider whether AI note-taking is appropriate. If you do use it, review transcripts for mistakes before sharing. Machines can still mishear or confuse details. This ensures that everyone's privacy is respected and that the information shared is accurate and reliable.

Many workplaces have policies on meeting recordings and data retention. Align your workflow with these rules: store notes securely, limit access, and delete transcripts once complete. Highly regulated or privacy-conscious organizations should consult IT or compliance teams before integrating new AI tools.

Combining AI efficiency with human oversight prevents misunderstandings. Skim AI-generated recaps before sharing to catch any errors. Double-check action items, including names and dates to ensure accuracy. When in doubt, add a personal note to clarify any details that may confuse.

Quick-Start Checklist for AI Meetings

- Choose an AI scheduling assistant (like *x.ai* or *Clara*) and sync it with your calendar.

- With consent, invite *Otter.ai* or *Fireflies* to your next meeting.

- After the call, check the AI-generated notes for errors.

- Share recaps with your team in their *Slack* channel or via email.

- Set reminders for action items using *Teams* task lists.

- Regularly audit bot access to your meetings and update permissions.

With the proper setup, these tools eliminate repetitive administrative work, allowing you to focus on real problems and project progress.

More Innovative Document Management with AI Search, Summaries, and Version Control

Suppose you've ever scrolled endlessly through a company drive looking for the latest contract draft or tried to remember where you saved last quarter's report. In that case, you know the pain of digital clutter. Most workplaces generate a vast array of documents, proposals, spreadsheets, PDFs, emails, and other digital content. Organizing, finding, and using this digital haystack can quickly drain your energy. That's where AI-powered document management steps in, and honestly, it's a game-changer once you see it in action.

Imagine searching for a specific file without needing to remember the exact title or folder. *Microsoft 365 Copilot* takes your plain language queries, like "show me the Q4 sales report we shared with legal last Tuesday," and cuts right through messy folder structures. Instead of sifting through endless filenames, you get direct links to the most relevant files, complete with previews and context. *Glean* amplifies this for larger organizations by searching not just files, but also messages, wikis, and project platforms. It understands context, so if you type "client contract with renewal clause," it surfaces documents where those words matter, not just where they're mentioned in passing. Semantic search like this means you waste less time clicking and more time doing what you need to.

Now, about those monster-sized reports that suck up half your afternoon to review. AI can shrink them down to size in seconds. With *Copilot* or similar tools, you don't have to read every line of a 50-page PDF. Instead, highlight the document, click 'Summarize,' and watch as key points and decisions appear in a concise brief that you can review over coffee. This isn't just helpful for reports; you can feed proposals, meeting notes, or even technical manuals into an AI summarizer and get the key points in a few bullet points or a short paragraph. For contracts and legal documents, you can pull out specific clauses with a straightforward search, such as "show me the indemnity clause" or "flag deadlines in this contract." AI tools look for the exact language or dates you care about, so nothing slips through unnoticed.

If you're prepping board packs or executive updates, AI-generated summaries help distill dense presentations into digestible overviews. You can double-check what the AI pulls out and add your spin or context before sharing, saving hours of manual effort while still keeping your voice front and center, no more missing key decisions buried on page 37; the AI finds them for you.

Keeping track of changes across multiple versions of a document used to mean color-coded edits and confusing email chains. Modern AI-driven version control tools make this so much easier. Let's say you're reviewing a contract that has received several rounds of feedback from different departments. *Kira Systems* compares versions side by side and highlights exactly what changed, down to single words or punctuation marks. It also flags places where two reviewers made conflicting edits or where someone rewrote a whole section without telling the group. Instead of guessing who changed what, you see it all at a glance.

This extends to any situation where collaboration occurs quickly, such as policy updates, marketing content, or even scientific papers. AI doesn't just track text changes; it suggests edits that smooth out awkward phrasing, catch repeated points, or spot missing information based on previous drafts. You receive more brilliant revision suggestions than a simple spellcheck has ever offered. Teams spend less time arguing about which version is "final" and more time improving quality.

Of course, working smarter with documents means being mindful of privacy and access. Confidential files need protection from prying eyes. AI tools can help, but only with the correct settings dialed in. Look for options that enable encrypted document processing; this scrambles your data during both storage and transmission, so only authorized users can view it. Most enterprise platforms let you set role-based access controls: only the finance team can open budget

spreadsheets, while legal gets exclusive access to contracts. When inviting collaborators, double-check permissions to ensure that external
guests can't access files they shouldn't be able to see.

AI can also audit who opens or edits sensitive files and alert you
if someone downloads too much data at once or attempts to share
it outside your organization. This adds a safety net against acciden-
tal leaks or malicious insiders. Always review your provider's privacy
policies and confirm data isn't used for training unrelated models
unless you give explicit consent.

If you're looking to implement these tools in your workflow, start
by mapping out your team's most significant time wasters, such as
searching for files, reviewing lengthy documents, or managing conflicting edits. Introduce one feature at a time so people don't feel
overwhelmed. Show quick wins, a before-and-after search demo, or a
summarized report that saves an hour, to build trust. And always back
up your data regularly; even with the most innovative tech, having a
good backup plan is non-negotiable.

The future of document management isn't about adding more
folders or stricter naming conventions; it's about letting AI do the
heavy lifting so you can focus on thinking, deciding, and moving work
forward with less friction each day.

From Lead Scoring to Campaign Copywriting using AI in Sales and Marketing

Suppose you've ever waded through a spreadsheet of cold leads. In that case, you know how much guesswork goes into figuring out which names matter. AI-powered lead scoring takes that grind off your plate. Instead of combing through every inquiry or contact, tools like *Salesforce Einstein* analyze past deals, customer interactions, and even email opens to predict which prospects are most likely to make a purchase. You open your dashboard and see leads ranked from hottest to coldest, with clear, data-driven reasoning behind each score. This means you can stop chasing ghosts and focus on prospects who are genuinely interested in talking. *HubSpot's* AI features take it a step further by tracking engagement, such as how often someone clicks your links, downloads guides, or replies to emails, and adjusting scores in real-time. You'll notice the sales team spends less time debating who to call next and more time closing deals. For niche or specialized industries, custom models enable you to create your ranking recipes. In your world, a prospect who attends webinars is gold, or someone who requests a sample kit is especially valuable. You can set those rules, feed them into the AI, and get a lead list that feels like it finally "gets" your business.

Moving past prospecting, AI shines when it's time to create campaigns that don't sound stale or generic. If you're not a natural wordsmith, this is where tools like *Jasper* and *Copy.ai* work magic. You plug in a few details, such as product name, target audience, and a key benefit, and the app generates product descriptions, ad copy, and even entire email sequences. Instead of staring at a blank page, you get ten options for a headline or call-to-action. Some of these tools even mimic your existing brand tone if you feed them samples of your past writing. The best part? When you need to personalize emails for different segments (such as new customers versus longtime fans), the

AI automatically adapts the content for each group. It can rewrite offers for various age brackets or tweak language for different regions, all in minutes.

Testing what works becomes less of a guessing game with the aid of AI. Picture running an A/B test on subject lines that were generated by the app itself. Instead of brainstorming five versions and hoping for the best, you create twenty in seconds, then let the system track which ones get opened most. The AI learns from past campaigns and keeps refining its suggestions with each send. For social media teams running numerous ads, this means you can keep things fresh without burning out from constant brainstorming.

Planning larger campaigns gets easier as well. AI-driven segmentation breaks your audience into meaningful groups based on real behavior, not just age or location, but buying patterns and interests. The tool might notice that people who buy one product tend also to read a specific blog post or share a particular type of social content. This insight helps you build customer personas that aren't just theoretical, they're based on what's happening in your data. When it's time to map the customer journey, AI will suggest next steps for each group, such as sending a special offer, inviting feedback, or nudging them toward another product.

Content calendars can transform from a headache to a helper with AI tools that scan for trending topics in your industry. They watch what's popular on social media or in news articles and suggest blog ideas or post schedules. Instead of scrambling for something timely every week, you receive a list of what's currently trending and when to publish for optimal engagement.

While it's tempting to automate everything, there's real risk in letting AI run wild with your brand voice. Machines don't instinctively know when a joke goes too far, or when a phrase feels off-brand or insensitive. Sometimes you'll find the AI suggests headlines that just don't fit your message, or worse, accidentally cross into cliché or stereotype territory. That's why human eyes should review every piece of content generated by an AI before it goes public. A quick gut-check saves embarrassment and keeps your messaging on track.

Brand safety needs special attention in automated advertising. If you're letting an AI write *Facebook* ads or *Google* campaigns, set strict guidelines on language and topics it can use (and what to avoid). Most platforms allow you to blacklist words or flag risky phrases so nothing problematic slips through. It's helpful to keep a short checklist handy: Does this ad align with our core values? Could it be misunderstood or offend someone? Would I feel proud sharing this myself?

The sweet spot is right where AI does the heavy lifting, sorting data, drafting initial versions, and surfacing trends, while your team polishes the final product and ensures every message honestly sounds like you. With the right balance, sales will find better leads faster, and marketing can generate more creative content with less stress, all without losing the human touch that makes people trust your brand in the first place.

Enhancing Presentations, Resumes, and Interview Prep with Job-Ready AI

Okay, you've just been told you need a slide deck for tomorrow's meeting. The deadline looms. Your mind races, but your calendar is packed. Instead of panicking or cobbling together mismatched slides, you turn to AI presentation tools like *Beautiful.ai* or *Canva Magic Design*. These platforms don't just hand over generic templates; they analyze your content, suggest layouts that fit your narrative, and pick color schemes that match your brand or topic. You drop in a few bullet points or a data table, and the AI instantly spins up polished, organized slides complete with impactful visuals. If you've got a spreadsheet of sales data or survey results, these apps can even generate infographics on the fly. Charts, icons, and images automatically pop into place, making your information more digestible without hours of fiddling. Say goodbye to endlessly aligning boxes or hunting for royalty-free photos; AI handles the grunt work so you can focus on your message.

Polishing your professional story isn't just about what's on the screen; it's about what lives on your resume and in your cover letter. The job market moves quickly, and sending out the same old document to dozens of job openings just doesn't cut it anymore. Resume assistants like *Rezi* and *Teal* take things to the next level. You paste the job description into their platform, and the AI scans it for skills, keywords, and requirements. Then it reviews your resume, flagging gaps and suggesting ways to tailor your experience to meet the employer's needs. If you're eyeing a career change or targeting a specific industry, this guidance is invaluable. The tools highlight missing phrases, recommend powerful verbs, and ensure your application passes through those pesky automated screeners that many companies use now. Cover letters get the same treatment, no more staring at a blank page. The AI drafts a personalized intro based on your background and the role, giving you a running start.

One innovative feature is keyword optimization. You have experience that matches the job, but you use different words than those in the posting. AI identifies these mismatches and suggests tweaks to ensure automated filters don't reject your application. For example, "client consultations" might be rephrased as "stakeholder engagement" if that's what the employer emphasizes. If you're missing a skill that's listed, such as *Excel* macros or bilingual fluency, the tool flags it, allowing you to address the gap honestly in your cover letter or prepare for questions in interviews. This isn't about gaming the system; it's about clear communication and giving yourself the best shot.

Landing an interview is only half the battle. Once that invite lands in your inbox, nerves can take over, especially if it's been a while since your last tricky question or video call. Here's where AI-driven mock interview platforms, such as *Interview Warmup* by *Google*, step in. These apps simulate real interview questions in your field, covering everything from technical know-how to tricky behavioral prompts ("Tell me about a time you faced conflict at work"). You answer out loud, and the AI listens, transcribes, and scores your responses based on clarity, structure, and relevance. Feedback lands instantly: maybe you used too many filler words, rambled off-topic, or missed a chance to showcase leadership. The system identifies weak spots, allowing you to refine your answers before facing a real interviewer.

Some tools even track non-verbal cues when you use video, flagging instances where you avoid eye contact (on camera), speak too quickly, or freeze up under pressure. Others let you replay your answers or compare attempts over time, helping you notice progress and patterns.

The first few tries might feel awkward, but it's much better to stumble in front of an AI coach than in front of a hiring manager.

Now, there's a real temptation to copy and paste whatever these platforms spit out, especially when deadlines press or confidence dips. But nothing turns off an employer faster than reading a cover letter that sounds like it was drafted by a bot or seeing a presentation with the same generic slide deck they've witnessed from ten other candidates. Avoid this trap by reviewing every AI-generated piece closely. Adjust the phrasing so it sounds like you, casual and friendly, with a crisp and direct tone. Don't settle for a bland, boilerplate response.

Let's ground this with a quick case study: imagine you're switching from education to project management. You feed both your old resume and the new job description into *Rezi* or *Teal*. The platform highlights where your teaching experience overlaps with leadership and planning skills required for project management, such as curriculum design (which aligns with workflow planning) or parent communication (client updates). It suggests adding bullet points about managing deadlines, coordinating with teams (including your students), and utilizing technology to track progress. You tweak the language further to make it authentic, no buzzwords for buzzwords' sake, and end up with a resume that tells your real story in terms employers understand.

The same principle applies to presentations and interview prep: use AI as your launchpad, but don't let it flatten your personality. Add anecdotes, tailor examples to each audience, and maintain a consistent tone that aligns with your personality. With the right mix of automation and authenticity, you'll stand out for all the right reasons, confident, prepared, and unmistakably yourself.

Bias Checks and Talent Matching Using AI for HR and Team Managers

Writing job postings often means double-checking every phrase for clarity and fairness. AI tools like *Textio* help by flagging coded or biased language, suggesting more inclusive wording to attract a broader and more diverse range of applicants. For example, phrases like "rockstar" or "digital native" are flagged for potentially excluding some candidates. This isn't about policing syntax; it's about ensuring you don't unintentionally turn away great talent. Performance reviews also benefit: AI-driven bias detection can analyze feedback to identify patterns, alerting you if certain groups consistently receive different types of praise or criticism, much like having a second set of impartial eyes.

AI also brings fairness to the candidate screening process. Human bias, even unconscious, can influence resume reviews. Tools like *E ightfold.ai* prioritize skills, experience, and potential, not traditional pedigree. The system surfaces matches based on abilities rather than names or schools, which helps you create more diverse and inclusive teams and accommodate non-traditional backgrounds. *Pymetrics* employs a science-based approach, utilizing brief, game-like assessments to evaluate cognitive and emotional traits. It then compares these results to your top performers, recommending candidates with similar strengths based solely on data, rather than relying on hunches.

Automated shortlisting steps up the process. Set filters, such as must-have skills or language fluency, and the AI narrows your interview pool to those who fit, regardless of factors like gap years or unknown colleges. The focus stays on what matters most for the job, not distractions. Yet, it's not about handing the process over entirely; it helps you spend less time filtering and more time engaging with top matches.

For current teams, tracking morale can be tricky, especially with dispersed or remote workers. AI-driven pulse surveys (e.g., *Culture Amp*) send quick, anonymous questions about workload, communication, or company changes. The AI analyzes responses for trends or warning signs, such as sudden spikes in damaging feedback or early indications of burnout. These are actionable insights that help pinpoint where management should engage in honest conversations.

Real-time sentiment analysis provides up-to-date feedback on projects, meetings, or communications, eliminating the need to wait for annual surveys. You get a stream of team sentiment, with positive and negative trends highlighted. Notably, this analysis is based on opt-in feedback, rather than surveillance, providing leaders with a more accurate understanding of current team dynamics.

Despite these advances, human oversight remains essential. Algorithms can't always catch the nuances behind a candidate's story or a performance dip. Managers should document how and when AI tools are used, specifically outlining the criteria applied, the assessments considered, and the process by which final choices were made.

This transparency is crucial for compliance and builds trust among employees and candidates.

Whenever AI influences hiring or evaluations, be transparent. Inform candidates that some steps are automated and explain the rationale behind this approach, emphasizing both fairness and efficiency. If asked, be ready to explain what criteria were most important and how the decision was made. This candor helps reduce suspicion and resentment.

Compliance can't be ignored. Regulations on automated hiring and data privacy vary by region, so it is essential to stay up-to-date. Ensure that candidates consent to automated assessments and have the option to opt out if they wish to do so.

How AI Supports Fair Talent Decisions

Visualize three layers:

- Job Ad Creation—*Textio* flags bias

- Candidate Screening—*Eightfold.ai* matches by skills, not demographics

- Team Engagement—*Culture Amp* monitors sentiment

- Human review is key at every step.

Adopting AI in HR is about automating repetitive tasks, allowing you to focus on talent and relationships, rather than replacing human judgment. As you incorporate these tools into your workflow, remember that transparency and empathy are just as important as efficiency.

In summary, AI can make work life smoother by facilitating hiring, team growth, and the processing of feedback. Next, we'll explore how leaders and individuals can use AI to handle broader workplace changes and future challenges.

Chapter Five

Achieve Business Breakthroughs by Adopting AI Without a Technical Team

Is Your Business AI-Ready?

So, you're in the office, coffee in hand, when someone asks if it's time to bring AI into your business. Before investing in new tools or consulting services, first determine if your business is genuinely prepared to benefit from AI. Like prepping a garden, without the correct foundational elements, even the best seeds (or AI tools) won't thrive.

Start with a readiness checklist. The first crucial step is to assess your digital infrastructure. Are your documents digital and stored in the cloud? Have you transitioned from email chains and spreadsheets to automated workflows? Suppose your team is still dealing with physical files or tracking sales on sticky notes. In that case, AI implementation will face immediate hurdles. A robust digital foundation is essential for AI projects, as it enables data to flow freely, allowing AI to analyze and provide valuable insights.

Next, evaluate the quality and accessibility of your data. AI relies on data, just as athletes rely on protein; it needs not just a lot of information, but clean, current, well-structured, and accessible data. Are customer records up to date and inventory lists accurate? Messy or inconsistent data can lead to poor results and headaches. Regular audits to eliminate duplicates, fill gaps, and standardize formats are crucial for achieving successful automation. Data hygiene, while not glamorous, is vital for AI's effectiveness.

People play an equally important role. The best tools are of little value if staff resist or fear change. Assess your team's willingness to embrace new systems. Is innovation seen as an opportunity or a threat? If skepticism prevails, start small and build trust and confidence with initial wins before expecting a complete transformation. Leadership must demonstrate top-down commitment and patience. Without re-alistic timelines and dedicated support, projects stall quickly.

Leadership support isn't just about words; it's about providing real resources, including a budget for tools, time for training, and permission to experiment. Both executive buy-in and support from departments directly affected by the changes are crucial, especially from those who will be using the new AI tools. Without this support, projects can quickly come to a standstill.

Here's a practical checklist to gauge readiness:

- Are your files and workflows mostly digital and cloud-accessible?

- Is your data organized, up-to-date, structured, and free from significant errors or duplicates?

- Does your workplace encourage learning and adapting to new technologies?

- Are leaders prepared to support AI projects with needed time, money, and patience?

- Do you conduct regular data audits and maintain clean data?

- Is staff trained to input clean, consistent data?

- Are there clear "AI champions" or points of contact in key departments?

- Do you have basic cybersecurity policies in place?

Data hygiene deserves special mention. Go beyond occasional spreadsheet sorting or deleting old files once a year. Establish regular audit routines, such as monthly or quarterly reviews, to identify errors, missing data, or outdated entries. Offer short training sessions for best practices in data entry, like using consistent formats and checking for anomalies. Clean data improves not only AI outcomes but also everyday business decisions.

Don't try to implement these changes alone. Identify and empower 'AI champions,' those who are excited by new tools and can effectively bridge the gap between departments. These aren't always managers; sometimes it's the go-to tech person or the colleague who's ready to test new apps. Assign project leads to keep initiatives moving and ensure clear communication. This approach will empower you and your team, knowing that dedicated individuals are driving the AI adoption process.

Include cross-functional stakeholders. AI isn't just an IT or management issue. It affects sales, customer service, logistics, and more. Involving different perspectives keeps expectations realistic and helps spot challenges early. This inclusive approach will make you and your team feel part of a collaborative AI adoption process, where everyone's input is valued and contributes to the initiative's success.

Address foundational issues before launching AI projects. If cybersecurity policies are unclear or outdated, address them first by establishing solid data privacy and access controls. Weak security can quickly lead to trouble as data becomes more valuable. And if business objectives for AI are fuzzy or uncertain, pause. It's essential to set specific goals, such as reducing manual tasks, streamlining processes, or gaining deeper customer insights, to ensure AI addresses real business problems.

If your assessment reveals significant issues, messy data, aging systems, or staff resistance, prioritize fixing those gaps. Rushing into AI without a sturdy foundation almost always leads to frustration and wasted resources. Taking time now sets the stage for smooth AI adoption later.

Quick-Scan Readiness Scorecard

Rate each from 1 (needs work) to 5 (rock solid):

- Digital infrastructure

- Data quality

- Staff openness

- Leadership commitment

- Cybersecurity

- Clear business objectives

Add up your points. If you score below 20, focus first on strengthening your foundation before adopting AI. Share your score with trusted colleagues and discuss top priorities.

Laying this groundwork means that when you adopt AI, it will address real problems and drive meaningful, measurable growth, instead of just being another passing trend.

Mapping Use Cases to Identify High-Impact Opportunities in Your Industry

You may be eager to see where AI can make a difference in your business. Still, the first thing to realize is that not every process benefits from automation or sophisticated algorithms. Start with a simple question: Where does the work feel stuck, slow, or just plain annoying? Grab a notebook or open a blank document. Walk through a typical week, jotting down every manual, mind-numbing, or error-prone task. Perhaps it's sorting emails in customer service, chasing late payments in finance, or handling endless paperwork in HR. Look for bottlenecks, places where tasks pile up or mistakes occur because people are overextended or systems aren't connected. This is your pain point map, serving as the best starting point for identifying innovative AI opportunities.

Once you've sketched out these trouble zones, think about which business functions they touch. Sales often gets bogged down by lead qualification and data entry. Operations can lose hours on inventory tracking or scheduling. Customer service lives in a world of repetitive questions and ticket triage. HR is overwhelmed by the volume of onboarding forms and the process of screening resumes. For each pain point, brainstorm how an AI-powered tool might help. In sales, AI can score leads based on past customer behavior, enabling your team to focus on the most promising prospects instead of making cold calls to everyone. In operations, AI can predict stockouts by analyzing orders and supplier patterns, keeping shelves stocked and costs down. Customer service bots can handle basic FAQs 24/7, freeing up staff for more complex issues. HR teams use resume-screening algorithms to surface top candidates or chatbots to answer common employee questions about benefits.

Each industry has its flavor of high-impact use cases. In retail, AI pricing engines automatically adjust prices based on demand, competition, and inventory levels; no more endless spreadsheet wrangling. Manufacturers utilize AI vision systems to detect defects on the production line before products are shipped, thereby reducing waste and returns. Healthcare clinics automate appointment reminders and insurance checks, cutting no-shows and billing headaches. Real estate offices feed property data into AI models to predict which listings will sell fastest or which neighborhoods are heating up. Even nonprofits benefit from donor prediction tools that identify likely contributors based on their giving history and campaign timing.

After listing possible use cases, it's time to prioritize them. Not every idea deserves your immediate energy or budget. Draw a simple two-by-two grid, feasibility on one axis (how hard is this to build or buy?) and impact on the other (how much time, money, or customer love will it save or earn?). Low-hanging fruit sits in the bottom right: easy to set up and delivers obvious value fast. These are your "quick wins," maybe automating invoice processing or setting up an AI-powered helpdesk. Projects that require extensive custom work or have uncertain payoffs (such as building a proprietary chatbot from scratch) are considered "moonshots." Mark these for later or when you have more experience under your belt.

To score each idea, ask a few key questions:

- How much manual time could we save every month?

- How many errors could we prevent?

- What would it cost to try this out as a small pilot?

- Are there affordable tools available, or would we need lots of custom development?

- Use a basic scoring system, such as high/medium/low or stars, and plot your candidates on the grid.

Quick-win pilots often involve high-volume, repetitive tasks with clear rules and procedures. If you can describe the process with "if this, then that," it's usually ripe for automation.

Don't let hype or FOMO (fear of missing out) drive your decisions. Align every AI project with actual business goals, cutting costs, speeding up delivery, boosting customer satisfaction, or increasing revenue. If an idea doesn't directly support a strategic priority, set it aside for now. The coolest chatbot in the world means little if your real issue is late shipments or employee turnover. Be brutally practical: Will this tool make life easier for staff? Will it improve the bottom line? If not, keep looking.

A common mistake is chasing AI for its own sake, buying into slick demos or buzzwords without a clear business case. Don't replace manual data entry with an untested AI that needs months of tuning and still makes mistakes; instead, look for proven tools that solve specific problems quickly. If you're unsure what constitutes "proven," check for testimonials from similar businesses or ask vendors for particular examples and references.

Consider starting with one department, such as accounts payable, that automates invoice scanning and matching. At the same time, everyone else maintains their usual workflow. Watch what happens: Does time free up? Are mistakes down? Is everyone happier, or just confused? Use these early results to build support for bigger projects. Share wins (and lessons from any stumbles) with the rest of the team.

Quick-Use Case Matrix

- Draw two axes:

  ○ Feasibility (easy-to-hard) on one side,

  ○ Impact (low-to-high) at the bottom.

- Plot your top five ideas as dots on the chart.

- Aim for quick wins, high impact, easy setup, before tackling anything ambitious.

Keep your focus on real-world outcomes and you'll avoid the trap of shiny but useless solutions. AI should always serve your business goals, not the other way around.

Choosing AI Vendors to Spot Real Value versus Marketing Hype

Selecting an AI vendor is crucial, and most providers will attempt to win you over with flashy claims and sleek presentations. That's why it pays to move deliberately and clarify what matters before allowing any new tool access to your data. Start by reviewing the vendor's track record. Focus on real-world case studies involving companies similar to yours, demonstrating measurable results, not just lofty promises or a logo parade. Insist on speaking with actual reference clients, not just curated testimonials. Request details on recent projects, honest feedback, and how challenges were addressed. If the vendor hesitates to provide genuine references or offers only generic, anonymous praise, be cautious.

Transparency is essential. A credible AI partner will explain their technology clearly, without burying you in technical jargon. If you ask, "How does this work?" or "What happens to my data?" and receive only vague or generic responses, take it as a red flag. What are the specifics? Do they utilize rule-based automation, machine learning, or another approach? If the answers are all hype with no substance, look elsewhere. Good vendors don't obfuscate; they're able and willing to break down their tools into understandable terms.

Customer support reveals a great deal about a company. Ask about the onboarding process: Will they guide you through it, or hand over a manual and leave you to figure it out on your own? Clarify what support channels are available and if you can reach a real person when needed. Discover how updates are managed and whether minor fixes incur additional costs. Favor vendors who offer helpful, ongoing support, those who listen when issues arise and consistently check in. Reliable support builds your team's confidence over time.

Beware of "AI-washing," slapping AI branding on any product. Watch for vendors who lean heavily on buzzwords ("AI-driven," "deep learning") yet provide no real explanations. If their materials rely on jargon and lack outcome specifics, be skeptical. Lack of independent reviews or third-party validation is also telling. If all endorsements come from their site, go further: check business forums and review sites to see if genuine users have seen measurable benefits.

Proof-of-concept (POC) trials are vital. Never commit to a long-term contract without first running a POC. Request a limited, real-world trial or a side-by-side pilot with your existing system to measure outcomes, such as reduced manual work or improved accuracy. Set clear criteria for success: if the tool doesn't meet specific benchmarks, don't proceed. A confident vendor will support this scrutiny and want their solution to prove itself outside a controlled demo.

Defining and tracking metrics is crucial. Before starting a trial, agree on the measures of success, be it response times, fewer errors, or hours saved. Collaborate with the vendor to closely track these metrics. If the vendor shies away from precise measurement or accountability, move on. You should never be left guessing about the value the tool brings.

Contracts are the decisive stage. Review all terms, particularly those related to data ownership and privacy. Your business data must remain yours, free from clauses that allow vendors to repurpose or sell it. Ensure details regarding data storage, security, and your rights to retrieve or delete data in the event the contract ends. Support guarantees should be explicit, including response times, included updates, and procedures if the vendor is acquired or ceases operations. Exit clauses are essential; ensure you can leave with minimal hassle and without incurring heavy penalties if things don't work out as planned.

Vendor Evaluation Checklist

- Does the vendor have relevant case studies and connect you to real reference clients?

- Do they clearly explain their technology, without using technical jargon or buzzwords?

- Is customer support thorough, with proper onboarding and ongoing assistance?

- Are there independent reviews or verifiable third-party results?

- Do they allow for a POC or free trial with your real data?

- Are success metrics defined and tracked throughout the organization?

- Does the contract safeguard your data and privacy?

- Is there a simple, fair exit clause if you need to leave?

These steps help you filter through the noise and select vendors who genuinely provide business value, not just flashy sales pitches, so you maximize your investment and minimize regrets.

A Step-by-Step No-Code Playbook to Launch Your First AI Pilot

Kicking off your first AI pilot doesn't require a tech army, just a clear plan and the right no-code tool. Think of it as giving your business a test drive with AI, no need to overhaul everything at once or tie up your budget in custom software. The trick is to pick a single, contained use case where you can see results quickly and measure them easily. For most teams, this means finding a workflow that's repetitive, prone to errors, or just plain tedious. Perhaps it involves sorting email requests, tagging support tickets, or processing invoices. The best pilots are those where success can be defined upfront, such as "reduce invoice processing time by 50%" or "cut manual data entry errors in half."

Once you've zeroed in on your target process, it's time to select a no-code AI tool that fits the job. Today's platforms are surprisingly accessible, with drag-and-drop builders and simple setup wizards. *Zapier*, for example, lets you automate repetitive tasks by connecting the apps you already use. *MonkeyLearn* offers text analysis features for sorting and tagging. *Power Automate* handles everything from email triggers to report generation with minimal fuss. The goal isn't to pick the fanciest solution, but rather one that you can set up without writing code or needing an IT team on standby. Most of these tools include free trials or demo accounts, so you can tinker before committing.

Before launching, set a baseline for comparison. Measure how long the process currently takes, how often mistakes crop up, and how much it costs in terms of staff hours or actual dollars. This provides you with concrete numbers to compare against once your pilot is operational. Please keep it simple: jot down average processing times, error rates, or any other relevant metric that makes sense for your use case. This isn't busywork, it's the only way to tell if your experiment works.

Every pilot needs a project manager, the person who owns the process from start to finish. This doesn't have to be a tech guru; pick someone who knows the workflow inside and out and isn't afraid to ask questions or rally the troops. Define each person's role early: who will set up the tool, who'll test it, who'll collect feedback, and who'll crunch the numbers at the end. Clear roles mean fewer crossed wires and less finger-pointing if things get bumpy.

Let's walk through a real-world example: automating invoice processing with an AI tool. Your accounts payable team spends hours each week entering invoice data into your accounting system, triple-checking totals, and chasing down missing info. You choose a platform like *Power Automate* to read incoming email attachments, extract data using its built-in AI model, and push everything straight into your finance app. Setup usually takes less than an afternoon. Connect your email inbox, map out the fields you want captured (such as invoice number, date, and amount), and run a few tests on sample files.

Kick-off starts with a team meeting. You demonstrate the tool and explain what will change (and what won't). Address concerns promptly. People fear that automation will break things or render their jobs obsolete. Open the floor for questions and invite honest feedback throughout the process. This isn't a one-way street; successful pilots depend on everyone feeling included and heard.

Run the pilot for a set period, such as two weeks or a full billing cycle. Encourage users to keep detailed notes about what works, what feels unusual, and any issues they encounter. Collect both informal comments ("This saved me thirty minutes!") and complex numbers (how many invoices processed per hour now versus before). At the end of the pilot, send out an anonymous survey asking about confidence in the new system, any unexpected time savings, or any headaches that arose. Staff buy-in often hinges on these small touches. A simple survey can surface resistance before it turns into bigger trouble.

Now comes the moment of truth: analyzing results. Compare your baseline numbers with post-pilot metrics. Did you save time? Are there fewer errors? If so, how much money did this free up? Sometimes improvements appear in unexpected ways, perhaps processing times didn't drop as much as hoped. Still, accuracy soared, allowing staff to focus on more important work. If things didn't go as planned, dig into why: Was setup confusing? Did data formats trip up the AI? Did staff need more training?

Don't rush to roll out anything company-wide until you've had honest conversations about what worked and what didn't. If gains are clear and everyone's on board, consider expanding the scope, such as automating other document types or bringing more users into the fold. If the results are mixed, adjust and try again with improved training or alternative processes. And sometimes the best move is to halt and reassess; not every pilot will be a smash hit.

The most effective pilots are those where communication flows freely, kick-off meetings set expectations, Q&A sessions tackle confusion head-on, and feedback is treated as fuel for improvement rather than criticism. When staff feel part of the process rather than subjects of it, they're far more likely to support new tools in the long term. It's not just about automating work, it's about building confidence one small win at a time.

Lessons from Failed and Successful AI Adoptions Help to Avoid Common Pitfalls

When it comes to rolling out AI in a business that doesn't have a tech team, things can get bumpy fast. I've seen plenty of companies jump in with high hopes, only to walk away frustrated and skeptical. Why does this happen so often? One of the biggest reasons is starting without a clear goal in mind. It's surprising how many AI projects begin with a vague idea, such as "let's automate something" or "we need to use AI like our competitors." Without a specific target, like reducing missed deliveries by 30% or speeding up response times for customer emails, it's impossible to measure success. I remember a local logistics firm that tried to use AI to "improve efficiency." They bought an expensive tool, but nobody could agree on what "improved" meant. Months later, the team was just as overwhelmed, and the software sat unused.

Insufficient data is another major culprit. AI requires clean, trustworthy data, or it produces nonsense. Take the story of a regional retail chain that wanted to predict which products would sell out next. Their sales data was riddled with duplicates, outdated SKUs, and missing prices. The AI kept flagging discontinued items as top sellers! Not only did this waste money, but it also eroded staff's faith in automated systems. If you feed your AI junk, don't expect gold in return.

People are just as important as technology. I've watched projects crumble because staff felt left out or threatened by new systems. One manufacturer introduced an AI scheduler without consulting the workers. They worried about layoffs and ignored the tool, sticking to their old routines. The project fizzled, and management blamed "bad technology." In truth, it was a people problem, change resistance at its core.

Expectations also get out of whack. It's easy to fall for flashy demos and think results will come overnight. I once helped a food distributor excited about a new AI inventory system. After a month, they complained it hadn't changed much, not realizing that these tools need time and fine-tuning. The real payoff requires patience and ongoing adjustments. Quick wins are possible, but significant shifts unfold over months, not days.

So, how do you avoid falling into these traps? Communication is your first line of defense. Get everyone involved early, not just decision-makers. Share what's coming, why it matters, and how it will help, not just the bottom line but day-to-day work. Regular updates help keep rumors at bay and increase buy-in. I always recommend hands-on pilot testing with real users from the start. Let them try the tool, poke holes in it, and give honest feedback. This not only spots issues early but also turns skeptics into supporters.

Celebrating small wins builds momentum. Maybe your AI system sorts invoices 15% faster after two weeks, shout it from the rooftops! Quick victories keep energy high and demonstrate to the team that progress is tangible, even if it's incremental. Sharing these results, both numbers and stories, turns abstract tech into something people can relate to and trust.

Ethics can't be an afterthought. Responsible use starts on day one. Set clear rules for what's fair game with data and how decisions are made by algorithms versus humans. Build regular checkpoints for reviewing outputs: Are recommendations fair? Is there any bias creeping in? If you're working with sensitive information, such as hiring or customer data, consider seeking outside opinions or consulting with legal experts to double-check compliance. Transparency goes a long way. If people know how and why decisions are made, trust grows naturally.

Let's look at a quick checklist you can use as a pitfall prevention tool:

- Is your data clean and current?

- Are stakeholders involved early and often?

- Have you defined what success looks like?

- Are you piloting before scaling up?

- Do vendors provide clear answers and take responsibility?

- Is there an ongoing ethics review process in place?

Now, for a brighter example: A small retailer wanted to cut down on product returns that were eating into profits. Instead of going big all at once, they started with a focused pilot, using AI forecasting to predict which items were most likely to be returned each season. They worked closely with store managers to clean up sales data and set realistic goals (reduce returns by 10% in three months). The pilot succeeded; returns dropped noticeably, and staff felt like they were part of the solution rather than sidelined by new tech.

Ultimately, making AI work for your business isn't about acquiring the flashiest tools or following trends; it's about setting clear goals, getting your team on board, staying patient through hiccups, and maintaining ethics at every step.

Pitfall Prevention Checklist

- Clean and maintain data regularly

- Involve staff early, gather feedback

- Define clear metrics for success

- Pilot before wide rollout

- Hold vendors accountable

- Schedule recurring ethics reviews

The businesses that thrive with AI aren't the ones that spend the most; they're the ones that plan carefully, listen to their people, and learn as they go. As you move forward with adopting AI, remember these lessons so your next step brings you closer to real, lasting improvements.

The next chapter will explore how to keep pace with AI advances and integrate learning into your work culture, ensuring these small wins continue without overexerting your team or budget.

Chapter Six

Your Living AI Learning Plan for Keeping Up Without Burning Out

Using Dashboards and Newsletters for AI Trends for Your Rapid-Update Companion

You're sipping your morning coffee, and instead of scrolling aimlessly through endless tech headlines or getting caught up in social media rabbit holes, you open your inbox to a neatly organized email that highlights only the most significant and relevant AI news from the past day, no endless search, no overload, just the good stuff, trimmed down and ready for you to use. That's the magic of "push" resources, those quick, curated updates that come to you instead of you chasing after them. When it comes to AI, where trends shift overnight and jargon multiplies faster than email spam, having these digestible sources is like having a personal research assistant who knows exactly what you want and delivers it on a silver platter.

If you've ever felt buried by the constant flood of articles, blog posts, and hot takes about artificial intelligence, you're not alone. Trying to keep up by constantly searching for updates is exhausting and ultimately less effective. "Push" resources, like dashboards and newsletters, take the burden off your shoulders by filtering out noise and delivering only what's worth your attention. These aren't just random collections of links; they're usually built or curated by experts who live and breathe AI. They read the firehose for you, then hand you the highlights, so you can stay informed without feeling overwhelmed or losing your free time.

Let's discuss what makes these resources stand out. Newsletters such as *MIT Technology Review's* "The Algorithm" and *DeepLearning.AI's* "The Batch" are must-haves if you want straight-to-the-point updates with zero fluff. "The Algorithm" zeroes in on practical breakthroughs, ethical debates, and big industry moves. At the same time, "The Batch" focuses on real-world applications and research that's shaping business and daily life. "Ben's Bites" is another favorite, offering fast, witty, and bite-sized takes on the latest product launches, funding rounds, and tool releases. "TLDR AI" does a fantastic job of boiling down complex news into quick summaries so that you can read a whole week's worth of developments in under five minutes. What sets these apart is trust; they're not just recycling press releases. They provide context, flag hype, and even alert you when something is overblown or requires a skeptical eye (Fast Company, 2024).

Dashboards take it a step further by letting you customize what you see. Imagine a control panel where you select the topics or companies that matter to you, such as generative AI for design, healthcare automation, or AI in education. Set up *Google Alerts* for specific keywords, such as "AI ethics," "small business automation," or "no-code AI tools." To set up *Google Alerts*, go to the *Google Alerts* page, enter your keywords, and choose the frequency and sources for your alerts. These alerts will land in your inbox as soon as something new pops up online. You can also use aggregator sites that track live updates from dozens of sources at once, sorting them by popularity, credibility, or relevance to your field. These sites, such as *Feedly* or *Flipboard*, enable you to create a personalized feed by adding sources and topics that interest you.

Customizing these updates takes just a few minutes but pays off for months to come. Most newsletters let you choose how often you want to hear from them, daily for real-time tracking, weekly if you prefer a big-picture view, or monthly for long-form analysis and trends. Dashboards usually have filters for industry focus; set yours to highlight news about retail or healthcare if that's where your work or interests lie. Don't be afraid to adjust as your needs change. For instance, if you're transitioning from a technical role to a managerial role, you might want to swap out technical updates for leadership and strategy insights. A new job might mean swapping out finance updates for education tools or adding alerts on responsible AI if you're moving into policy work.

Once those updates start rolling in, make it a habit to scan headlines first. You don't need to read every article top-to-bottom; look for stories that jump out as directly relevant. Skim the summaries if something seems immediately useful, such as an announcement about a new tool that could save your team hours; flag it right away. When you come across deeper dives or think pieces that spark curiosity but aren't urgent, pin or bookmark them for weekend reading or your next lunch break. This approach keeps your daily workload light while still giving you space to explore big ideas when you have more time.

Fast-Filter

Block five minutes each morning (or whenever suits you) to review your chosen dashboards or newsletters. In round one, scan headlines only, star or highlight any that feel relevant. In round two, read just the summary for those starred items. Pin one "deep dive" article each week for further reading, and schedule it into your calendar like an appointment with yourself. This fast-filter exercise not only keeps you updated but also saves you time, allowing you to focus on what's most important in your day.

By leveraging these push resources (expertly curated newsletters and customizable dashboards), you'll swap stress and FOMO for a steady stream of insights that fit your schedule, rather than letting them run your life. This way, staying sharp on AI becomes a habit, not a headache.

How to Pick the Right AI Apps for Your Needs with Curated Toolkits

Building your own AI toolkit begins with being honest about what slows you down or frustrates you on a day-to-day basis. Maybe it's the endless back-and-forth of scheduling meetings, or the mountain of reports you never seem to finish. Some folks get stuck on messy notes, while others drown in repetitive emails. Before you even think about shiny new apps, jot down your biggest workflow headaches. Don't sugarcoat it. If invoice sorting, managing your calendar, or writing blog posts makes you groan, put it on the list. Once those pain points are out in the open, you can match each with a tool that solves a specific issue, not just adds another icon to your home screen.

It's tempting to grab every trending app or "AI-powered" service that pops up on *Product Hunt* or social media, but chasing quantity over quality is a recipe for digital clutter. Instead, focus on picking tools that work together and genuinely lighten your load. For writing and brainstorming, *ChatGPT*, *Jasper*, and *Notion AI* all shine in different ways. For example, *ChatGPT* is great for generating quick ideas or engaging in conversation, *Jasper* excels at crafting punchy marketing copy, and *Notion AI* seamlessly integrates into your notes and documents without causing disruption. If you want to boost productivity, *Motion* can build a dynamic daily schedule around your real priorities. *Mem* acts as a smart personal knowledge base, and *Otter.ai* transcribes meetings so you never lose track of decisions. For visual work, *Canva* and *Beautiful.ai* enable you to create polished presentations and graphics in minutes, even if you have no design experience.

Before you commit to any tool, put it through a quick "pilot before you pay" trial. Most quality apps offer a free version or at least a limited trial so you can see if it fits your style or adds noise. Take a week actually to use it with a real project or task; don't just click around. Does it save time? Is the interface friendly, or do you get lost after two clicks? Can you export your work easily? Transparent pricing is a must. If you can't find the cost after five minutes of hunting, consider that a red flag. Also, review cancellation policies to determine if there are any hidden fees associated with the features you need.

Privacy should never be an afterthought when picking AI apps. Always check what data the tool collects and how it's stored. Look for clear privacy policies. If it reads like a legal maze, that's a warning sign. See if there are options to limit data sharing or keep information on your local device. Community reviews can be gold here, search for posts or comments from real users describing their experiences with bugs, billing surprises, or customer support headaches.

To keep things simple, here's a checklist when assessing new apps:

- Can you try it for free?

- Is pricing up front and fair?

- Is setup painless?

- Are privacy settings precise and customizable?

- Does the tool play nice with your existing software?

- And finally, do actual users have good things to say?

Suppose an app ticks most boxes but leaves you uneasy about one area, especially security or data handling. In that case, it's usually smarter to pass.

Over time, it's easy to accumulate too many tools after trying every new thing that comes along. This "shiny object syndrome" sneaks up slowly until your workflow is more complicated than before. To fight it, set a reminder every three months to review your toolkit. Open each app and ask: Have I used this in the last month? Did it help? If not, uninstall or cancel it. Less really is more when every tool earns its place.

I once worked with someone who started using more than ten different AI apps daily, including one for notes, another for writing, two separate calendar tools, and three design platforms, among others. Their digital life was chaos. After an honest review and some tough choices, they cut back to just three essentials: one for writing (*Notion AI*), one for scheduling (*Motion*), and one for presentations (*Canva*). The result? Way less confusion, faster task completion, and an easier time training team members who didn't need to memorize a dozen logins.

If you're building your toolkit, start small and personalize it as you go. Perhaps all you need is *Otter.ai* for meetings, plus *Canva* for client proposals; maybe *ChatGPT* handles your brainstorming, while *Motion* keeps your schedule under control. The point isn't to keep up with every new launch but to pick what genuinely fits your needs, and then actually use those tools until they become second nature. Keep your workflow tight by reviewing regularly and letting go of apps that aren't pulling their weight.

AI App Decision Quick-Scan

- Have I defined my pain points clearly?

- Does this tool directly solve one of those problems?

- Is there a free trial or demo available?

- Are costs and cancellation terms easy to find?

- Do I understand (and control) what happens to my data?

- What do real users say about reliability and support?

- Is my toolkit getting bloated? (Review quarterly, keep only what works.)

A smartly chosen toolkit streamlines the tech clutter, so AI feels like an ally, not another source of stress, in your daily routine.

Harnessing Infographics, Cheat Sheets, and Mind Maps for Visual Learning

Nothing sticks quite like a good visual. Ever try to explain how a chatbot works and see eyes glaze over in the room? That's where a sharp infographic or a sketch on the back of a napkin makes all the difference. If you're like me, you probably find yourself remembering a diagram long after a wall of text fades away. Visuals have a sneaky way of making complex ideas, such as the flow of data through an AI model or the steps in training a neural network, feel less intimidating. It's kind of like having a map on a road trip, except you see every turn before you get lost. When I stumbled onto my first mind map of machine learning, connections between topics jumped out at me. Suddenly, "supervised learning" didn't float as an isolated buzzword; it hooked directly to real-life stuff like spam filters and voice assistants.

If you're not already using infographics, you're missing out on one of the easiest ways to cut through confusion. Imagine an entire process, such as how your bank's chatbot determines whether your question is about your account balance or a lost card, broken down in a single glance. That same information might fill three pages of text, but one well-made chart does the trick in seconds. Sites like *Visual Capitalist* whip up eye-catching graphics that turn data into stories, while *Towards Data Science* and *DataCamp* are goldmines for process overviews and cheat sheets. I've found that even official documentation, such as *OpenAI's* guides, now includes more diagrams and visual summaries. Finally, tech companies are catching on that most of us want to see how things work without hunting for a computer science degree.

You don't need fancy software or art skills to make your mind maps or annotated screenshots either. Start with a blank piece of paper or an app like *XMind* or *Miro* if you want to go digital. Say you're learning a new AI tool, write the tool's name in the center, then branch out with bubbles for setup, key features, everyday tasks, and any gotchas you spot along the way. Keep the branches short and sweet: "Data import," "Automated reports," "Security settings." Use arrows to connect steps that flow together, or different colors to group related features. If your mind wanders while reading documentation, stop and sketch each step as you go. You'll be surprised at how quickly patterns form and gaps in your understanding become apparent.

Screenshots might seem basic, but they're powerful learning tools when you add notes. The next time you walk through a workflow, like setting up an AI-driven calendar, take a screenshot at each significant step. Open those images in *PowerPoint*, *Google Slides*, or even *Paint* and layer on arrows, highlights, and simple captions ("Click here to sync Google Calendar"). This makes a step-by-step guide you can re-visit anytime or share with others who need help. For larger processes, stitch screenshots together vertically to create a visual checklist for future reference.

Infographics aren't just personal cheat codes; they also have real value for group learning. If you're leading a team meeting or running a workshop, print out your go-to visuals and post them around the room for easy access. People will glance at them even when they're not paying full attention (and those images will stick). I've seen teams use laminated process maps taped by their desks as quick references for things like chatbot troubleshooting or new project kickoffs. Visual guides reduce the number of "How do I do this?" questions, especially for new hires.

Don't forget digital sharing. Annotated diagrams slot perfectly into *Slack* channels or group chats when someone needs a reminder, or when you want to keep everyone on the same page for a new workflow rollout. Drop a mind map into your team's *Google Drive* or *Notion* hub so it's always handy before a big launch or quarterly review. Some folks even use visuals as checklists: cross off each step of training an AI model or setting up an integration as you go so nothing slips through the cracks.

DIY Mind Map Quickstart

Pick one new AI tool this week and make a quick mind map of its functions: center bubble for the tool's name, four main branches (Set-up, Features, Best Use Cases, Common Pitfalls), then sub-branches with details from your first test run. Snap a photo and pin it above your desk or upload it where your team can see it.

When learning about AI or teaching it to someone else, visuals unlock understanding in ways that text can't match. They shrink big ideas down to digestible bites, build bridges between scattered concepts, and make knowledge stick around much longer than dry notes ever will. Whether you're leading a meeting or just teaching yourself something new on a slow afternoon, infographics and mind maps will be your secret weapon for making sense of this fast-changing field.

Myth vs. Reality in Building Critical Thinking About AI Claims

The world is noisy with big promises about artificial intelligence. It feels like every tech article, sales pitch, or workplace brainstorm includes some bold claim about what AI will do next. You've probably heard everything from "AI will take all our jobs" to "this tool will make your business ten times faster overnight." If you want to keep your sanity and make wise choices, you need a filter, not just for hype, but for good old-fashioned nonsense. That's where critical thinking comes in. Instead of taking every statement at face value, you can use a simple mental checklist to spot red flags and separate fact from fiction.

Whenever you come across a claim about AI, whether it's a new product that says it "learns like a human" or an article predicting robots will run everything soon, pause and ask: "Does this claim cite real-world evidence?" If the only proof is a buzzword or a fancy graph with no source, that's your cue to dig deeper. Ask yourself, "Who benefits if I believe this?" Is it a vendor trying to close a sale, a journalist hunting for clicks, or someone in the office eager to look cutting-edge? Spotting the motive behind a message helps you distinguish marketing spin from genuine breakthroughs. When a company describes their system as "revolutionary," I like to press for details: Has anyone outside their PR team tested it? Are real users sharing results? If those answers are missing, skepticism is your friend.

Let's debunk some of the most common myths alongside the current reality. Take the idea that "AI will replace all jobs." The truth is far more layered. While automation has made specific roles less common, think toll booth operators or data entry clerks, most jobs change rather than vanish. Workers often find themselves performing various tasks, including those that require judgment, empathy, or hands-on troubleshooting skills that machines have not yet mastered (Gartner, n.d.). Even in manufacturing, where robots have been around for decades, people are still needed for oversight, creative problem-solving, and adapting when things go awry. Another favorite myth: "More data always means better results." In truth, good data beats lots of messy data every time. Feeding bad information into an AI tool yields faster mistakes; think of it as turning up the volume on the wrong song. The quality, relevance, and cleanliness of your data matter much more than sheer size.

Fact-checking is your superpower. When you hear something wild, maybe an AI model "predicts stock markets flawlessly" or claims to diagnose diseases better than doctors, look for supporting evidence. Cross-reference claims with industry groups known for independent research. The Partnership on AI and the Alan Turing Institute both publish honest reports about AI's strengths and weaknesses. Academic sources are gold here; *Google Scholar* lets you search research papers and studies to see if experts back up a claim or if it's just marketing smoke. Regulatory bodies sometimes also weigh in. Check if there are policy papers or guidelines addressing the claim in question. If you find three or four reputable sources that agree with each other, chances are it's grounded in reality. If not, keep those red flags up.

Healthy skepticism isn't about being cynical; it's about remaining sharp and open-minded at the same time. I try to model this by saying, "I don't know, let's find out together," whenever someone throws a bold statement my way. If a vendor claims their tool utilizes "cutting-edge neural networks" to save your department hours every week, ask them to provide evidence from real customers. Request case studies or references; you can contact directly. If they dodge the question or drown you in jargon, it's probably time to move on. Sometimes I'll even ask myself, "What evidence would change my mind on this?" That question keeps me honest and curious, rather than just defensive.

Imagine a scenario: You're in a meeting and someone says a new AI tool can "think like a person" and will solve all your team's problems if you sign up now. Before getting swept up, slow down and ask some pointed questions. Who else has used this? What did they accomplish? Can we test it before committing? Who stands to gain the most if we believe this right now? Create space for disagreement and don't be afraid to admit uncertainty. That's where real learning starts.

Spotting Hype vs. Reality

- Does this claim include real-world evidence (case studies or testimonials from actual users)?

- Are there any external sources that also convey similar messages?

- Who benefits most if I accept this claim?

- Is there independent validation (research paper or regulatory guidance)?

- Am I being pressured to act fast without time for review?

- What would convince me this is true?

Approach AI claims with curiosity and a sense of humility. The field moves fast, but hype moves even quicker. Your ability to pause, question, and check sources will save you headaches and help you make smarter decisions every single time.

Finding Your Community Using Online Groups for Support and Networking

Trying to learn a new AI tool by yourself can be frustrating, but you don't have to do it alone. Online communities make learning and growth much easier. These groups aren't just for tech experts; they're filled with a diverse mix of people, including parents, teachers, freelancers, and more, all sharing tips, celebrating wins, and helping each other troubleshoot. There's comfort in knowing you can ask questions, read others' discussions, or observe and learn. Sometimes, seeing someone else ask what you were wondering unblocks your progress, and returning the favor is rewarding when you're able.

Peer support is invaluable. Suppose you encounter a bug or are unsure how to automate a task. In that case, crowdsourcing solutions from individuals with firsthand experience is much quicker and less stressful than sifting through documentation or outdated videos. These networks also motivate you. Watching others share their AI projects or workarounds makes it clear that incremental progress is

more important than perfection and that everyone gets stuck sometimes.

Choosing the right group matters. For professional, structured interactions, *LinkedIn* hosts active groups, such as *Women in AI* and
the *Data Science Society*, both known for their welcoming culture and
genuine networking opportunities, think webinars, mentorship, and
personalized job leads. Suppose you prefer straightforward conversations and honest reviews of tools. In that case, Reddit's *r/Artifi-
cialIntelligence* is full of real talk, lively debates, and beginner-friendly
posts. Non-coders exploring automation can check out *r/NoCode* for
practical workflow ideas. *Slack* and *Discord* servers, such as *Data Talks
Club* or *Indie Hackers*, bring together hobbyists, professionals, and
founders in chat-style spaces, offering everything from quick advice
to in-depth technical discussions. To meet people in person or locally,
Meetup.com lists AI-related events, workshops, and hackathons.

Joining a new group can feel intimidating. Don't rush to post,
lurking is fine and helps you get a sense of the group's culture, see
which questions receive quick answers, and learn about popular topics. Review threads to determine what's on topic, and when you're
ready to join in, start small by introducing yourself or commenting on
someone else's post. When seeking help, be clear about what you've
already tried, e.g., "I'm stuck syncing *Notion AI* with my calendar;
here's what I've done" to get the most useful replies.

Good questions matter. Explain your problem, mention resources
you've already checked, and share what outcome you want. This helps
others help you and shows respect for their time. If you solve a problem, even a simple one, share your results; what's evident to you may

be exactly what someone else needs. Don't let worries about expertise hold you back. Communities thrive when everyone shares their unique experiences and perspectives.

With multiple groups on various platforms, notifications can get overwhelming. Set boundaries, mute channels you don't need, check in at set times, or opt for digest emails rather than live alerts. It's fine to dip in and out; you don't need to read every post. The goal is to have reliable help and inspiration available when you want it.

Beyond daily messages, these communities unlock opportunities you'd rarely find alone. Virtual hackathons, webinars, and collaborative projects provide hands-on learning and global networking opportunities from the comfort of your desk. Many groups offer job boards, mentorship, and practical collaboration opportunities for individuals from diverse backgrounds, not just technical experts. Members often form connections that lead to interviews, mentorship opportunities, or valuable feedback. Even if you're not chasing a career change, being part of a group helps you stay motivated and less isolated as you learn.

To sum up: staying up to speed with AI doesn't mean going it alone or grinding harder. Community support turns confusion into clarity, keeps you moving when motivation dips, and connects you to helpful people and opportunities. As the book shifts to ethics and building confidence, you'll see these relationships remain valuable well beyond the excitement of learning new tools.

Chapter Seven

Case Studies and Sector Blueprints for Real-World AI in Action

Healthcare Heroes Using AI for Diagnosis, Scheduling, and Patient Insights

Did you ever walk into a doctor's office, look around at the sea of paperwork, and think, "There must be a better way"? Healthcare is one of those places where you want everything to work seamlessly, where minutes matter and mistakes aren't an option. AI isn't just changing the rules here; it's quietly saving lives, time, and sanity behind the scenes. Imagine you have a loved one waiting for test results. Now, picture an AI system reviewing that MRI scan alongside the radiologist, double-checking for anything subtle that could be missed by tired eyes.

Across hospitals from Boston to Bangalore, AI algorithms are boosting diagnostic accuracy in ways that would have seemed outlandish a decade ago. *Google Health's* AI tools for reading X-rays and MRIs are now catching signs of diseases like breast cancer and tuberculosis earlier and more reliably than ever before. These systems ingest countless medical images, learning to spot the faintest hint of trouble, a shadow on a lung, a tiny nodule in breast tissue. Not only do they alert doctors to what matters, but they also help reduce "false negatives," meaning fewer missed diagnoses. It's like having a superhuman second opinion at your fingertips. *Zebra Medical Vision's* platform performs a similar function, flagging potential fractures or early signs of osteoporosis in bone scans, enabling doctors to intervene sooner.

Even in dermatology, AI is moving from the lab to your pocket. Skin cancer detection apps now allow you to snap a photo of a mole or spot with your phone. The app then compares your image to thousands of others, highlighting features that could indicate melanoma or other skin conditions. While these apps don't replace a real dermatologist, they give you an early warning, sometimes the difference between easy treatment and a much more challenging road ahead.

Chronic illness doesn't take a day off, and neither do the new wave of wearables. Smartwatches and fitness bands aren't just counting steps anymore; they constantly monitor heart rhythms, oxygen levels, and sleep patterns. Suppose you have a parent with diabetes or heart issues. In that case, AI-powered remote monitoring can catch warning signs before anyone feels symptoms. These devices alert both patients and doctors to spikes or drops in vital signs that might mean trouble. That means fewer emergency trips and more peace of mind for families.

The headache of hospital scheduling is a genuine concern. Double-booked appointments, endless hold music, and last-minute cancellations —it's enough to make anyone want to give up. Predictive scheduling software steps in here, crunching historical data to project which slots are most likely to be filled or missed. Hospitals use this info to overbook just enough (without chaos), maximizing efficiency and reducing those long waiting room marathons. On the patient side, AI-powered chatbots send appointment reminders by text or email, answer simple questions, and even help you reschedule if something comes up. This reduces no-shows and distributes the workload among staff, allowing them to focus on actual care instead of making endless phone calls.

Digging through mountains of patient data used to be a slow and overwhelming process. Now, natural language processing (NLP) tools sift through electronic health records at lightning speed, pulling together trends or red flags that even sharp-eyed researchers might miss. Hospitals can utilize these insights for a range of purposes, from clinical trials to refining care protocols. Real-time warning systems represent another significant leap forward: AI connects live sensor data from hospital beds, including heart rate, blood pressure, and breathing, to identify patterns that suggest patient deterioration before it becomes critical. Staff get an early heads-up so they can act fast.

Of course, no tech comes without hiccups. Data privacy is a significant concern in the healthcare industry. AI works best when it has access to large datasets, but patient records are highly sensitive. Strict regulations, such as HIPAA in the U.S., combined with technical safeguards like encryption and anonymization, help keep information secure; however, breaches and misuse have still occurred. Another challenge: bias in medical datasets. If an AI is trained mostly on data from one group, say, middle-aged men, it might miss symptoms common in women or people of color. This isn't just theoretical; there have been real cases where AI systems underperformed for specific populations because their training data wasn't diverse enough. That's why leading hospitals now stress inclusive datasets and ongoing review, ensuring that everyone is considered in the system's development and use.

Human oversight remains non-negotiable. There was a widely reported case where an AI flagged a chest X-ray as cancerous when it was actually a harmless anomaly. Luckily, an experienced doctor caught the error before treatment began. These stories remind us that AI is brilliant at pattern recognition but not infallible. Physicians use AI as a tool, not as a replacement for their expertise, and always check its recommendations before making critical decisions. This emphasis on human oversight should reassure you of the system's reliability and instill confidence in its use.

Take a Moment

Take a moment to think of your most recent healthcare experience. Was it marked by paperwork overload or long waits? Jot down how you'd imagine AI could improve just one piece of that process for you or your loved ones. Would you trust an AI-powered diagnostic tool if your doctor explained how it works? Why or why not?

With every advance, healthcare demonstrates that AI isn't about replacing people; it's about providing professionals with the proper support when accuracy matters most.

Financial Frontlines Using AI in Fraud Detection, Risk Analysis, and Personal Finance

Have you ever received a call or text from your bank about a suspicious $200 transaction at a distant gas station? That relief you feel when fraud is caught early is likely thanks to AI. Behind every "Did you authorize this purchase?" message, machine learning models tirelessly scan billions of transactions to spot anything unusual. Major banks and payment companies like *Mastercard* use platforms, such as *Mastercard's Decision Intelligence*, that track your spending habits, create a digital fingerprint of your "normal," and flag odd activity. But AI's role in finance goes beyond fraud detection and risk analysis. It's also a powerful tool for personal finance management, helping individuals track their spending, set budgets, and make informed financial decisions. Suppose your card is used simultaneously in two cities or you suddenly spend a significant amount on electronics you never intended to buy. In that case, the system picks it up instantly. AI's always-on detection protects your money whether you're awake or asleep.

Fraud detection now relies on speed and accuracy without hassling honest shoppers. Traditional methods used pages of rules, triggering too many false alarms. Machine learning, by contrast, learns from real cases to detect evolving scam patterns, employing techniques like n-grams to analyze sequences of spending actions and spot anything that doesn't fit your usual "story." It doesn't just watch for big-ticket items; sometimes, a series of small odd purchases signals fraud, too. Banks and fintechs can respond in seconds, freezing charges and contacting you right away. Even newer fintech startups utilize these tools to establish trust from the outset.

For loans and credit cards, AI is streamlining and aiming to make processes fairer. Rather than wait weeks for human review, algorithms often handle the initial assessment. They review your credit score and income, but also tap into alternative data, such as rent or utility payments and patterns in your digital life (with your consent), helping those with thin credit files get a fair shot. Small businesses, in particular, benefit from AI robo-advisors, which quickly analyze cash flow and expenses to recommend loan products tailored to their specific needs. Approvals that once took days can now happen in hours. By reducing human bias, such as a loan officer's subjective judgments, AI opens opportunities for more people.

Yet, not every decision should be handed over entirely to machines. The "black box" issue looms: if an algorithm declines your loan, you deserve an explanation. Sometimes, not even the bank staff can clarify why, as only developers may fully understand the model. Regulators now demand transparency. In Europe, GDPR grants you the right to an explanation for automated decisions that affect you. In the U.S., agencies like the CFPB require financial firms to involve humans and clearly explain denials. Striking the right balance between speed and fairness is still ongoing work.

On the personal finance front, AI money management tools are getting smarter. Budgeting apps like *Cleo* and *You Need a Budget* (YNAB) do more than monitor spending; they also forecast upcoming bills and suggest ways to stretch your money, utilizing predictive analysis to warn you when you're approaching your limit. The more you use them, the better they understand your habits, sometimes even flagging forgotten subscriptions.

Investing has also become more accessible with the aid of AI. Robo-advisors like *Betterment* and *Wealthfront* automatically rebalance your portfolio as markets change. If one sector grows too fast while another lags, the system adjusts the balance, taking into account your risk tolerance and long-term goals. While returns aren't guaranteed, these services help prevent mistakes such as panic selling or overconcentration.

AI has also improved round-the-clock banking support. Advanced chatbots now answer basic questions, process disputes, and handle tasks like transferring funds or sending payment reminders at any hour, no more waiting for business hours or navigating phone menus.

Still, AI isn't flawless. Algorithmic bias can creep in if models are trained primarily on data from a single group or region, leading to misjudgments in other contexts, such as undervaluing certain income types or misinterpreting different spending habits. Banks must continually audit their models, including language-based features, and keep systems updated. Regulators require fairness audits and demand clear explanations for how decisions are made. Consumers benefit most when institutions commit to ongoing transparency and model testing.

If you're interested in how your bank uses AI, ask questions. Many providers now share high-level guides explaining their fraud detection and loan decision models. The most trustworthy institutions are transparent about their privacy practices, fairness, and the operation of their systems. They don't just ask for trust; they show their work.

Manufacturing and Logistics Using AI for Inventory, Routing, and Predictive Maintenance

Factories and warehouses, once noisy halls where every breakdown triggered a scramble, now run more like well-tuned orchestras thanks to AI. Imagine a world where machines not only tell you when they're tired but predict when they'll need a break before anything actually goes wrong. This is predictive maintenance in action. Picture a conveyor belt rolling along in a bottling plant. It's equipped with IoT sensors that continuously monitor for unusual vibrations, track temperature, and measure speed. All this data feeds into innovative software trained to spot the warning signs of a failing bearing or motor long before a human would sense trouble. Instead of waiting until the whole line grinds to a halt, these systems shoot off an alert: "Replace part X in three days." That means fewer emergency repairs, less downtime, and massive savings, because, let's face it, nobody likes scrambling for spare parts in the middle of the night. *GE's Predix* platform is a solid example. It collects streams of sensor data from turbines, pumps, and motors across industrial plants, running advanced analytics to forecast exactly when maintenance crews should take action. This predictive power keeps everything running smoother and slashes those surprise costs that used to eat up budgets.

Inventory headaches haunt everyone from small retailers to global mega-stores. Running out of stock at the wrong time or discarding expired goods are both expensive problems. AI is now the brain behind inventory optimization, making sure shelves and bins are stocked just right. Instead of relying on gut feelings or last year's trends, AI systems utilize real-time inputs, including sales patterns, weather data, social media buzz, and even traffic flows near stores. For perishable goods—think fresh produce or baked items, AI crunches numbers to predict demand spikes or lulls so nothing sits too long and goes to waste. Retailers can set up dynamic reorder points that shift automatically, triggering new shipments only when it makes sense. This reduces both shortages and overstock. In big-box stores and e-commerce warehouses, dynamic pricing also plays a role. Suppose a particular product isn't selling quickly enough. In that case, the AI nudges prices down just enough to encourage sales and make room for what's currently in demand.

Logistics might sound like a boring word, but in reality, it's the backbone of getting everything from your toothpaste to your favorite snacks delivered on time. Here's where route optimization really shines. Delivery companies like Amazon and UPS feed their fleet data, driver locations, traffic jams, weather forecasts, into AI-powered planners that map out the most efficient paths for every van and truck. These algorithms don't just look for the shortest distance; they juggle delivery windows, package sizes, local restrictions, and driver hours.

The software can even adjust in real time if there's an accident on a main road or a sudden storm. For last-mile delivery, the complicated stretch between warehouse and your doorstep, AI finds clever shortcuts that save fuel, lower emissions, and get your package to you faster.

Inside massive distribution centers, AI takes charge of cross-docking (moving goods directly from receiving to shipping with little or no storage) and coordinates fleets of autonomous robots. These bots zoom around aisles picking orders, restocking shelves, or shuttling items from one dock to another. The AI keeps everything in sync, so robots don't collide or double-handle products, resulting in less wasted motion and fewer mistakes.

Of course, none of this happens without people adapting right alongside the machines. As AI takes over repetitive diagnostics or automates the manual route planning process, the workforce is also changing. Workers who once spent days manually checking machines now learn to interpret predictive maintenance dashboards or troubleshoot sensor networks. Upskilling becomes part of daily life; technicians acquire new skills in data analysis and system calibration, rather than just wrench-turning. Companies are rolling out on-the-job training programs so maintenance crews can read AI-generated reports and act on them confidently rather than feeling threatened by technology.

A significant shift is underway with collaborative robots, often referred to as "cobots." Instead of caging off robots for safety, teams work side by side with these intelligent helpers. Cobots are capable of performing heavy lifting or repetitive assembly tasks. At the same time, humans handle quality checks or intricate functions that still require a careful touch. The result is fewer workplace injuries and higher overall productivity without anyone feeling replaced. Some companies bring in "AI champions," employees who enjoy tinkering with new technology, to bridge the gap between old routines and the latest tools, showing others how these changes actually make their workday easier.

This transformation isn't always easy or automatic. It requires honest communication from managers about what's changing and why, as well as support for those who need extra time to adapt. When employees have the opportunity to work with AI instead of against it, they're more likely to view these tools as partners rather than threats.

Quick Reference Infographic

Imagine a single-page cheat sheet pinned on a breakroom wall: Sensors feed live data into AI dashboards → Predictive alerts for maintenance pop up before breakdowns → Smart inventory systems adjust stock based on real-time trends → Dynamic route planners keep delivery fleets moving efficiently → Cobots team up with humans for safer, faster work on the floor.

In modern manufacturing and logistics, AI isn't about replacing people; it's about building more intelligent systems where each player (human or machine) can do what they do best without wasting time or effort.

Creative Industries Using AI in Design, Writing, Video, and Music

You've probably seen wild, futuristic posters or slick product ads online and thought, "Who makes these?" The answer more often now is: a creative person working side-by-side with AI. In design, AI has become a turbocharged co-worker that never gets tired, always suggests new color palettes, and can whip up a logo draft in seconds. *Adobe's Creative Suite* now incorporates AI into everything from retouching old photos to generating custom layouts based on a few simple sketches or prompts. Generative design isn't about robots replacing designers; it's more like having a digital brainstorming partner who never runs out of ideas. With just a few clicks, you can ask the AI to mix up your composition, stretch or shrink elements, or invent a dozen new versions of a logo for you to tweak. Sometimes it even spots visual quirks you'd miss after staring at the same image for hours.

Writing content for ads, blogs, or social media used to mean staring at a blinking cursor waiting for inspiration. Now, tools like *Canva's Magic Write* step in to draft catchy marketing copy, suggest engaging headlines, and even rewrite sentences to match different moods, formal, playful, urgent, or calm. It's like having an editor who doesn't sleep but still cares about your voice. Instead of spending hours on the perfect sentence, you get three or four options to riff on. The magic is in the mix: your ideas plus AI muscle equals more content, faster, without losing your unique style.

In the realm of video and music production, the role of AI is expanding at a rapid pace. Automated video editors, such as *Descript* and

RunwayML, can instantly transcribe spoken words, cut out awkward pauses, and even remove background noise with a single tap. Imagine shooting a quick how-to video for your business. AI can add subtitles, generate translations for new audiences, and crop the footage to ensure it looks good on every social platform. Film students and indie creators utilize these competent editors to refine their cuts in minutes, rather than days. For music makers, AI tools like *AIVA* and *Amper Music* whip up custom soundtracks and jingles with just a prompt (think "jazzy morning energy"). You tweak instruments and tempo till it feels right. That's not all; AI can blend genres or mimic playing styles, allowing you to experiment without hiring a full band.

Deepfake technology is another wild twist. While it raises eyebrows, it's also being used in creative ways, such as seamlessly swapping actors' faces for visual effects in movies, generating voiceovers in any language, or creating ad campaigns starring digital "influencers." Still, this stuff comes with big questions around trust, ethics, and what's "real." The same tools that can entertain or localize content can also mislead or manipulate if not handled transparently.

The legal side of creative AI is currently a maze. Who owns an image made by an algorithm? If you use an AI-generated song in a commercial, do you pay royalties, or does nobody get paid? Lawsuits have already begun regarding whether training an AI on millions of artworks or songs constitutes "fair use" or copyright infringement. Some courts have ruled that only humans can own copyrights, while others continue to debate what constitutes original versus derivative work. Attribution has also become a hot topic: many platforms now require creators to disclose when AI was involved and to credit the tools used. If you're using AI for business projects, be aware of this potential legal gray area, as it could lead to headaches down the road.

Artists and writers are experimenting with these new tools every day. Illustrators using *Midjourney* or *DALL-E* describe the process as half painting, half prompting —a back-and-forth where the machine fills in broad strokes, and they tweak details until the image feels "theirs." Musicians sample AI-generated loops to build new tracks that would've taken weeks to compose from scratch. Writers use story generators as plot sparring partners. One novelist I spoke with runs her outlines through an AI chatbot to stress-test dialogue or brainstorm new twists when she hits a wall.

One YouTuber I know automates every step of her video creation process: subtitles are generated in real-time (saves hours), translations reach fans in Spain and Japan in minutes, and AI even suggests cut points for *TikTok* shorts based on audience retention statistics. She told me that the most significant shift isn't just the time saved, but being able to focus on the creative choices that matter most without getting bogged down in repetitive, mundane tasks.

Case Study Profile

Meet Alex, a digital artist who blends *Midjourney's* AI sketches with hand-drawn overlays for his comic book series. He starts by prompting the AI with his character descriptions ("gritty detective with neon jacket in rainy city"), then pulls the generated images into Photoshop. There, he adjusts colors, sharpens outlines, and adds custom touches that only make sense in his story's world. Alex credits the AI as a "jumpstart," a way to shortcut the blank page phase while still making every panel his own.

Creative industries aren't trading away originality; they're expanding possibilities by incorporating AI into their processes. The magic still happens at human hands; AI hands over more raw material for you to shape into something truly yours.

Education and Nonprofits Using AI for Personalized Learning and Social Good

Picture a classroom where every student gets exactly what they need, no one left to drift and no one bored, waiting for others to catch up. This isn't some wild fantasy; AI-powered adaptive learning platforms are making it real. Tools like *DreamBox* and *Squirrel AI* don't just repeat old lessons; they also provide new insights. They monitor how each student is answering, spot patterns in mistakes, and then adjust the next question or activity in real time. Maybe Jamie breezes through fractions but stumbles on decimals; the platform quietly shifts focus, offering more practice where it's needed most. This active tailoring enables teachers to support twenty or thirty kids at once, each one on their own unique learning path. For students who often get lost in the shuffle, this kind of precision can help close achievement gaps that previously seemed impossible. Even language learning is getting a significant boost, especially for those in underserved communities. Chatbots now serve as tireless tutors, engaging in conversations that are both informative and engaging, answering grammar questions and offering feedback on pronunciation, all without judgment or fatigue. These bots can bring English lessons to rural villages or help kids in crowded city schools practice at their own pace, anytime.

Outside the classroom, nonprofits are utilizing AI to address some of the world's most pressing challenges. Public health organizations can now predict disease outbreaks days or even weeks in advance, compared to traditional methods. With AI platforms like *BlueDot*, data from airline ticket sales, news reports, and weather feeds are analyzed to spot early warning signs of illnesses spreading across borders. When COVID-19 began to spread around the globe, it was an AI system that identified the pattern before most governments did. Disaster response has also been transformed by AI's ability to process satellite imagery at scale. After hurricanes or earthquakes, organizations like the UN World Food Programme use machine learning to scan thousands of images for damaged roads and buildings. This enables them to map out safe routes for aid trucks or identify which neighborhoods need help first, thereby shaving precious hours or days off the response time.

AI isn't just about high-tech heroics; it's transforming how nonprofit teams manage their daily workload. Grant writing, often a marathon of research and copy-pasting, now gets a jumpstart from AI assistants that draft basic proposals or pull relevant statistics from massive databases. This doesn't mean humans are cut out of the loop; it means that overworked staff can focus on strategy and relationships instead of getting bogged down in paperwork. Fundraising is also becoming more innovative with the use of AI. Donor segmentation tools sift through giving histories, flagging supporters who might be ready for a personal call or a special campaign update. Instead of sending one-size-fits-all emails, organizations can tailor messages that actually resonate, resulting in better outcomes and less wasted effort.

All this progress comes with big questions about fairness, transparency, and community voice. If only a handful of wealthy schools or charities can afford these tools, the gap between haves and have-nots could widen even more. That's why there's a growing push for open-source AI platforms, tools anyone can use, adapt, or improve without paying massive licensing fees. Some nonprofits take it a step further, inviting local communities to help label training data so that algorithms reflect real needs and cultural context, rather than just numbers on a spreadsheet. This kind of collaborative approach also builds trust; people are more likely to accept an AI-driven decision when they've had a hand in shaping it.

Keeping things transparent matters too. If an adaptive learning system decides a student is "struggling," teachers and parents deserve to know why, not just see a mysterious score. Many schools and nonprofits now demand explainable AI, platforms that show their work and offer clear reasons for every suggestion. When families, educators, and donors understand how decisions are made, it becomes easier to identify bias, correct mistakes, and keep everyone moving toward the same goal.

Take a Moment

Think about a cause or a classroom you care about. Where do you see routine work bogging people down? Jot down two tasks that could be made lighter or more personal with the help of AI, maybe automating a monthly report or offering quick language tips to new arrivals. Now, imagine what the freed-up time could mean for real people: more face-to-face connections, deeper conversations, or simply less stress at the end of the day.

AI's role in education and nonprofits isn't about replacing heart or passion; it's about removing barriers so that more energy can be devoted to teaching, caring, and making a lasting impact. As we look ahead, it's clear that the most effective uses of AI will always prioritize people, amplifying what humans do best while ensuring that no one is left behind.

Wrapping up this chapter, you can see how AI isn't just for big businesses or high-tech labs; it's also making an impact in classrooms, community centers, and relief efforts worldwide. The next step is to understand what it means for your own skills and plans, and how you can prepare yourself to thrive as these tools become part of everyday life.

Chapter Eight

Navigating AI Ethics, Bias, and Emotional Intelligence

The Bias Checklist for Spotting and Reducing Algorithmic Bias

Let's begin with a familiar scenario: you apply for a job online, upload your resume, and wait. What you don't see is an AI system likely sorting your application before a human ever does. Suppose that the system was trained on resumes mostly from one type of background. In that case, perhaps an algorithmic bias related to a particular gender, school, or city is at play. Algorithmic bias occurs when AI systems make decisions that unfairly favor or disfavor certain groups, typically due to biased or incomplete training data or flawed assumptions embedded in their design. Even systems that seem neutral can reinforce real-world inequalities unless carefully managed (IBM, n.d.).

At every phase of AI, bias can creep in, from data collection to rule-making to outcome prediction. For example, collecting data from just one neighborhood or making design choices based on limited perspectives means the output may not treat everyone equally. Bias most often starts at the data level. If some groups are missing or under-represented, the AI can't fairly evaluate everyone. Model design also plays a role. For instance, if developers overemphasize specific skills or use proxies like ZIP codes, the system's decisions might skew based on factors that correlate with race or income, introducing unfairness that's not always visible.

Empower yourself with the knowledge that you don't need deep technical know-how to spot problems or ask thoughtful questions about an AI tool you're using at work or in daily life. Use this practical bias checklist: Start with, "Who collected this data?" If it's from a narrow group, bias is likely. "Who's missing?" If people like you or others aren't represented, outcomes may be skewed. "What outcomes are being measured?" Does the tracking benefit only some groups? Finally, look for unexplained gaps in results between demographics; if certain groups consistently get worse results, that's a significant warning. Don't hesitate to press vendors or decision-makers for details about data sources and evaluation methods.

To reduce bias, even if you're not a coder, advocate for regular data audits in any AI system your organization uses. Push for ongoing bias testing to compare outcomes by age, race, gender, and other relevant factors; even fundamental spreadsheet analysis can highlight missing representation. Include people from diverse backgrounds and departments during reviews to catch blind spots. In meetings with vendors, demand transparency on model training and testing for fairness, and if possible, choose tools that allow easy data review and adjustment. Remember, ongoing oversight is key to maintaining the fairness of AI systems, providing reassurance and security.

To illustrate, consider these quick stories. First, a company found that its AI resume screener was less likely to advance women in hiring. The investigation revealed that the model favored resume styles and keywords more commonly associated with men, reflecting historical biases rather than actual ability. The fix was retraining with more balanced data and removing gendered language from scoring. In another case, a credit algorithm used ZIP codes to predict risk, excluding people from predominantly marginalized neighborhoods from loan approvals—even when they were financially qualified—removing ZIP code as a factor led to fairer results.

Your Bias Checklist

- Who collected the data used by your AI tool?

- Who is missing from the dataset?

- What outcomes are being measured, and who benefits?

- Are there unexplained differences in results across groups?

- Does the tool support regular audits and adjustments?

- Are decision makers open about how their algorithms work?

Use this checklist when evaluating or rolling out any AI feature, even with everyday tools. It helps identify early problems and encourages essential conversations about fairness and inclusion. Bias in AI isn't always immediately apparent. Still, with curiosity and a willingness to challenge assumptions, you can help make AI systems fairer for everyone.

What Every User Should Know About Data Privacy in the Age of AI

Every day, we interact with technology that quietly collects details about our lives. Smart speakers listen for commands, and sometimes more. Fitness trackers monitor your steps, sleep, and even your heart rate. Location apps track your movements, creating incredibly detailed maps of your routines. This is your digital data trail, an invisible record traveling from your devices to the cloud, where companies store, analyze, and sometimes share or sell your information. Every time you use an AI-powered device or service, you provide it with personal data, often without being aware of it.

AI thrives on data. These systems learn from your routines, preferences, and even moods by processing patterns in your behavior. This can make life more convenient, with services like predictive text, personalized playlists, or weather alerts. It's important to remember the positive potential of AI in enhancing our daily lives, even as we navigate its privacy implications. Still, it also raises critical questions about who sees your data and how they use it. Some AI tools anonymize data, stripping away names and identifiers, while others keep more details than you might expect. Companies may retain your data long after you've deleted an app. Terms such as "data retention" (the duration for which your information is stored) and "third-party sharing" (companies sharing your data with partners, advertisers, or sometimes unknown entities) frequently appear in privacy policies. Yet, their true meanings are usually buried in the fine print.

Privacy policies and consent forms should protect you, but they're typically written in dense legal language that discourages careful reading. Still, it's worth scanning for key information: How long is your data retained, and who has access to it? Be vigilant for vague phrases like "may share with trusted partners" without specifying who those partners are, as this may be a warning sign. If opting out or deleting your information requires jumping through multiple hoops, that's another red flag. Good privacy policies should plainly state if they use encryption, anonymize your data, and provide clear instructions for opting out or deleting information.

Empower yourself by being proactive in managing your data privacy. Start by adjusting privacy settings on every AI device or app you use, and choose the strictest options—Disable location tracking when it's not essential for app functionality. Regularly check which apps have access to your calendar, contacts, and camera, and revoke unnecessary permissions. Favor services using end-to-end encryption for sensitive messages or personal info. Don't hesitate to delete unused accounts or request data removal from apps you no longer use; many companies now provide dashboards that let you review and clear your collected data.

Practical Checklist for Users

- **Disable location services** except when necessary

- **Regularly review app permissions** and revoke those not required

- **Enable encrypted backups** for your key data

- **Use private browsing/incognito mode** for sensitive searches

- **Delete unused accounts** and request complete data deletion

- **Set reminders** to review periodically and precisely store data

Global privacy laws have significantly shifted users' rights. Europe's GDPR and California's CCPA, for example, require companies to clearly explain their data practices and enable you to demand deletion of your data. The "right to be forgotten" exists; you can request that an app or network erase your personal information from their servers. While exercising this right may involve persistence and communica-

tion, these protections are enforceable. International companies gen-
erally comply to avoid fines or negative publicity.

Understanding the scope of data collection isn't about paranoia;
it's about taking control of your digital footprint. The next time an
AI-powered app requests broad access to your device or accounts,
stop and ask: Does this seem reasonable? Am I truly comfortable with
where this data could go? If not, don't hesitate to deny permissions or
look for more privacy-conscious alternatives.

AI's Role in Empathy and Emotional Intelligence for Humans and Machines

Sometimes, you want to be understood. You can spot genuine
empathy in a friend's voice, a coworker's supportive message, or even a
quick nod in a tough meeting. Now, picture an AI chatbot trying to fill
that gap. The difference is stark; machines don't feel, they calculate. AI
can analyze words and even pick up on patterns in your writing. Still,
genuine emotional intelligence remains outside its reach. Sentiment
analysis, the tool AI uses to "read" emotion, works by scanning for
keywords and phrases. It might see "I'm fine" as neutral, missing the
heavy sarcasm or sadness hiding underneath. In customer support,
this leads to awkward moments: you fire off a sarcastic complaint,
the chatbot cheerfully replies with a canned apology, and you're left
feeling unheard.

Developers have started to bridge this gap by teaching AI to detect
or react to emotions. Consider chatbots that scan messages for signs

of frustration. When they detect words like "angry" or "disappointed," they may escalate your case to a human agent. In education, AI-powered tutors notice when a student's answers become erratic or their messages turn terse. The system then shifts its tone, offering encouragement or simpler hints. These systems utilize massive datasets, comprising millions of conversations, to identify patterns that suggest someone is experiencing distress or is experiencing a mental block. It's clever, but still shallow. The machine doesn't care; it simply knows what response is statistically likely to be helpful.

This raises important ethical questions that shouldn't be ignored. When machines begin to mimic empathy, they can blur the distinction between genuine understanding and programmed responses. If you've used apps like Replika, you may have noticed how easy it is to fall into conversations that feel almost real. For some individuals, especially those who feel isolated, these interactions can be comforting; however, there's a risk of over-relying on AI for emotional support. Chatbots designed to persuade or influence behavior might even manipulate users' feelings for profit or power. In mental health, this is especially tricky: an AI might offer soothing words but miss signs of severe distress or risk.

To use AI "empathy" wisely, you need some guardrails. Any AI chatbot or mental health app should act as a supplement, not a substitute, for human connection and professional care. If a conversation turns serious or emotionally charged, it's time for a real person to step in. Set boundaries by utilizing these tools for surface-level support, such as reminders, journaling prompts, and motivation, while always encouraging follow-up with friends, family, or counselors when things get tough. In customer service, push for companies to offer clear options to reach a human when you're not getting the help you need from the bot.

Think about this reflection prompt: Would you want a friend or loved one to get comfort only from an app during their hardest moment? Probably not. Machines can simulate concern, but their understanding is limited to pattern-matching and probability. Social context, shared experiences, and genuine empathy remain firmly within the realm of humanity. Use AI as an assistant for basic support or routine check-ins; don't let it become your only lifeline when connection matters most.

AI will continue to improve at sounding warm and supportive, which can be particularly helpful in certain circumstances, such as triaging low-level problems or motivating students on a challenging day. Just remember that beneath the friendly tone is code, not care. When you see chatbots "reading" emotion and adjusting their replies, it's all about statistical patterns, not real feelings. In moments where nuance matters, such as grief, conflict, and deep frustration, lean on people who can read between the lines and respond with genuine understanding.

When using any emotionally intelligent AI tool, keep transparency front and center: companies should disclose when you're chatting with a bot instead of a person, and users deserve clear information about how their feelings may be analyzed or stored. Use these tools intentionally and maintain a strong social safety net by reaching out to real people for meaningful connections and support whenever possible.

Transparency and Explainability in Making AI Decisions Understandable

Ever received a decision from a company, like an unusual insurance rate or a loan denial, and thought, "How did they decide that?" That's where AI explainability matters: how clearly an algorithm shows its reasoning. In AI, explainability means opening the hood, making the system's logic visible so that people can follow the reasoning, instead of just accepting the answer. People often mention "black box" models, where the logic is hidden and even experts struggle to clarify how decisions are made. By contrast, "glass box" models provide transparency: they lay out the main steps or factors that shaped the decision, making it much easier for those impacted to understand and question the outcome.

This distinction is critical. Imagine an AI-powered system determining your car insurance premium. If the company can't explain which details, like your driving record, zip code, or car model, mattered most, you remain in the dark. When AI impacts your finances, employment, healthcare, or personal liberties, you deserve more than "the computer says no." You should receive an explanation you can follow. That's not just about fairness; it's about accountability and trust. The more understandable the process, the more likely people are to accept and benefit from the results.

Fortunately, understanding AI outcomes doesn't require a tech background. Many organizations now employ tools that simplify complex logic into plain language or visuals. For example, you may see a dashboard summarizing which factors most influenced a decision: maybe "recent claims" added $80 to your premium, while "good credit history" subtracted $40. Some firms use interactive flowcharts that let you trace how specific data influenced decisions. These explanation tools are rapidly improving, making it possible for non-technical users to see, not just the outcome, but the reasoning behind it.

You can hold a company accountable by asking pointed questions: "How did your AI reach this decision?" or "Can I see what influenced my result?" Most vendors should provide at least a basic breakdown, including plain-language summaries, key factors, or visual representations of the decision process. Larger organizations might keep audit trails, logging every step the AI took so that you can challenge any result. If you get vague responses, that's a prompt to push further or escalate.

Some organizations stand out for their approach to transparency. One hospital implemented an AI tool to prioritize patients in the emergency room. Still, staff were wary of trusting a machine with urgent decisions. Leadership prioritized transparency: for each patient, the system displayed which symptoms and test results were most critical, allowing doctors to review or override its recommendations. This fostered trust and improved outcomes because clinicians understood when and why to rely on the AI.

In finance, a credit union's AI-driven loan approvals initially left customers confused and discontented by unexplained rejections. Instead of hiding behind jargon, the company began including clear breakdowns with each letter: "Your application was affected by three missed payments last year and a high balance on one account." Clients then understood what to improve, and satisfaction rose, as people felt respected, even if the answer wasn't what they wanted.

Decoding AI Logic

Imagine a flowchart: your data enters, including income, payment history, and credit length. Each stage is split, illustrating how every factor influences the decision in one direction or the other. At the bottom, the outcome (approved, denied, or proposed rate) connects back to key influences. These visuals empower you, turning confusion into something you can question or act on.

As AI shapes more decisions in daily life and business, ask for explanations you can understand. Transparent systems not only protect your rights, they foster trust and fairness by making the rules visible. And that's something everyone should expect, every time.

Leading Ethical AI Initiatives Using Decision Trees and Risk Assessment Tools

When you're staring down the decision of whether to use AI for a new business process or a community service, it can feel a little like being dropped in the middle of a maze with signposts written in a language you don't speak. The good news is that ethical risk assessment doesn't need to be shrouded in mystery or reserved for tech gurus. I've found that using a clear, step-by-step framework makes all the difference, especially if you're leading a team, running a department, or want to ensure your project does good rather than harm. Imagine a flowchart in your mind, one that starts with a simple question: "Does this AI touch people's lives in a way that could help or hurt?" If the answer is yes, or even maybe, you move to the next branch: "Could vulnerable groups be affected?" Then: "If something goes wrong, can we reverse it?" And finally, "Is there someone clearly in charge of making things right?" Each of these checkpoints guides you, pausing you before you rush into automation that could carry hidden risks.

I always recommend pulling out a risk matrix before launching any new AI-driven feature. It doesn't have to be fancy: draw two axes on a piece of paper, one for how likely something is to go wrong, and the other for how bad the fallout would be if it did. Plot possible problems, such as data leaks, unfair results, or unintended consequences. Anything that lands in the high-likelihood, high-impact square requires immediate attention and likely further discussion. This visual tool helps you see at a glance what needs more controls or backup plans. Alongside this, create a checklist for stakeholder input. Did you invite feedback from people who might use or be affected by the AI? Did you involve community representatives, customers, or employees from diverse backgrounds? Community consultation isn't just box-ticking; it's about surfacing blind spots early and making sure your tool is fit for real life.

Ongoing oversight is where many projects stumble, but it's what separates one-off fixes from lasting improvement. The best teams set up regular ethics reviews, sometimes holding informal meetings and sometimes formal "red teams" dedicated to identifying risks and challenging assumptions. These groups aren't there to block progress but to ask tough questions and propose safer options. Anonymous whistleblower channels can also be a game-changer. People are far more likely to speak up early about problems if they know they won't face blowback. Make it easy for anyone, staff, users, or even customers, to flag suspicious behavior or poor outcomes. Encourage sharing feedback and establish processes to act on it promptly.

Let me share a couple of quick stories that drive home why this matters. One tech company had ambitious plans to roll out an AI-driven customer support bot. Just before launch, someone on the team flagged that the system often misunderstood messages from non-native English speakers, sometimes giving rude or unhelpful replies. Instead of pushing forward and hoping for the best, leadership hit the pause button. They brought together language experts and customer reps to test and tweak the system until it treated everyone respectfully. That short delay saved them from embarrassing headlines and frustrated customers down the road.

On another front, a nonprofit was co-designing an AI tool to aid in housing access. Rather than building in isolation, they insisted on working with community members who'd faced housing insecurity themselves. These individuals identified early flaws, such as confusing forms and questions that felt intrusive. They helped shape an AI that was both effective and compassionate. The result? People trusted the tool because they saw their voices reflected in its design.

"Should We Use AI Here?"

Picture this chart taped above your desk: Start with "Will this AI affect people's opportunities or wellbeing?" If yes, ask "Can we explain and reverse decisions if needed?" If not, rethink or redesign. Next: "Have we talked with those most affected?" If no, schedule those conversations now. Only when every branch ends in clear accountability and ongoing review do you move forward.

Ethical AI isn't an afterthought; it's an everyday practice built into planning, launch, and beyond. Decision trees and risk matrices might sound basic. Still, they're powerful tools for anyone who wants not just more innovative systems but kinder ones too.

Case Studies in Responsible Innovation Show AI for Good

When you see headlines about AI, it's easy to think of robots taking jobs or chatbots running wild. But beneath the noise, there are stories where AI is a real force for good, quietly changing lives and communities for the better. Think about wildfire prediction systems that crunch satellite images and weather patterns to warn first responders hours before flames reach neighborhoods. These systems save homes and sometimes entire towns, giving people a chance to evacuate or firefighters more time to act. Or picture a classroom where deaf students watch their teacher on screen, and real-time captioning appears as the lesson unfolds. That's AI bridging a gap, making education accessible to everyone, no matter their hearing ability.

The most inspiring projects consistently share a few key charac-
teristics. First, there's a spirit of openness, where ideas, code, and
results are shared without being locked behind expensive licenses.
Open-source AI efforts in humanitarian aid are a great example. Developers, nonprofits, and volunteers collaborate on tools to analyze
disaster photos after hurricanes or earthquakes, enabling relief agencies to send help where it is most needed. It's not just about the technology; it's about people from all over the world pitching in. Another
key ingredient is transparency; groups like the Partnership on AI have
published best practices for responsible development, pushing teams
to document their methods and invite feedback from outside experts.
These frameworks aren't just guidelines; they're blueprints that make
sure ethical choices are woven into every step.

Sometimes, even well-meaning projects hit unexpected bumps. I
recall reading about an AI system designed to guide a significant storm.
At first, it mapped flooded areas using drone images and suggested
where to send food and supplies. But a few weeks in, volunteers noticed supplies weren't reaching some smaller neighborhoods. A quick
review revealed that the AI had missed these spots because there was
insufficient data from those areas, no recent photos, or reports. Rather
than scrapping the project, the team brought in residents to help flag
missing regions and retrained the model. The fix wasn't instant, but
it built trust and led to better results. It's a powerful reminder that
community involvement and humility are as crucial as fancy code.

There's also so much potential in education. AI literacy programs
offer students in underserved schools new ways to learn, such as adaptive tutors that adjust lessons or recommend extra exercises based on
each child's individual needs. These tools level the playing field for

kids who might not have access to after-school help or private tutors. Still, the best results come when teachers and families join the process, suggesting tweaks and sharing what works.

If you're curious about getting involved, you don't need to be a coder or data scientist. Many organizations actively seek volunteers with a wide range of skills, from helping explain complex technology in plain language to testing new features or spreading the word locally. Try reaching out to groups like DataKind, which connects professionals with social impact projects, or join open-source communities on platforms like *GitHub* that focus on disaster relief and accessibility. Even pitching an AI-for-good idea to your local nonprofit can spark something big. Start with a simple outline: What problem could you solve? Who would benefit? How might AI help? Offer to help connect them with resources or experts if they want to explore more.

Responsible innovation is a team sport. The best projects are transparent from start to finish, invite participation from those affected, and continually learn from both successes and setbacks. As you consider AI's role in your life or work, remember these stories - proof that innovative technology, when paired with collaboration and heart, can truly make a difference.

Ending this chapter here, I hope you feel encouraged by what's possible when AI is done with care and purpose. Next, we'll explore how to future-proof your skills and mindset, ensuring you thrive regardless of how rapidly technology evolves around you.

Chapter Nine

Future-Proofing Your Skills and Mindset

Future-Proofing Your Career by Identifying Skills AI Can't Replace

At a block party, you engage in a conversation about the increasing role of technology in automating routine tasks at work. The discussion takes a turn when the focus shifts to the unique human abilities that are irreplaceable in the workplace. The consensus is clear: the future of your career is anchored in your human-centric skills, not just in flashy tech skills.

Let's clarify which skills will keep you ahead, regardless of how so-phisticated technology becomes. Complex problem-solving tops the list. Say your team confronts a supply chain crisis or a client's quirky demand, AI can crunch data and recommend options. Still, it strug-gles to grasp the full context or measure ethical implications. Humans connect the dots, weigh the consequences, and make judgment calls in ambiguous situations. This capacity for nuanced decisions is unique-ly ours. Critical thinking goes hand in hand; it's about questioning assumptions, evaluating evidence, and perceiving layers beneath the obvious. Where a bot might misinterpret outliers or sarcasm in a customer's email, you notice inconsistencies and ask, "What's missing here?"

Emotional intelligence and interpersonal communication are not just corporate jargon. In a world of automated emails and digital chatter, your ability to read subtle cues and respond with empathy is what truly distinguishes you. You have the power to defuse tense situ-ations with a well-timed joke or a reassuring word. Machines may send polite replies, but they can't build trust or truly mend relationships. Your human touch is irreplaceable, whether you're guiding a colleague through change or reading the unspoken mood of a room.

Creativity and originality are not just desirable; they are essential. Whether you're brainstorming a campaign or rethinking a process, AI can recombine existing knowledge to inform new insights. Still, it can't spark the radical new ideas that drive breakthroughs. It's humans who notice fresh patterns and make improbable connections, the kind that shape art, business pivots, or inventive solutions. These creative flashes are what make us distinctly human, and they are the fuel for progress and innovation.

Lastly, ethical judgment and leadership remain firmly in human hands. AI executes prescribed rules and optimizes for preset goals. Still, when facing difficult decisions, such as dividing scarce resources or handling private data, it's human integrity and fairness that set the standard. Leadership is more than delegating; it's about modeling honesty, transparency, and ethics. People turn to a human leader for direction when answers aren't obvious.

Self-Assessment and Targeted Growth

Take ten minutes to journal about a recent tough decision, at work or in life:

- Which factors did I weigh that weren't just data points?

- How did I adjust my communication for different people?

- Where did I introduce fresh ideas or refine existing ones?

- What personal values influenced my decision?

For a deeper insight, role-play challenging conversations, such as a tough negotiation or customer complaint, with a friend, then switch roles and reflect on what came naturally and what was tough.

Real-world stories highlight the value of these skills. A nurse might use software for rare diagnoses, but still relies on judgment and bedside manner to comfort anxious patients. A marketer can leverage analytics but succeeds by crafting a resonant story, not just following the numbers. Similarly, a teacher can use AI for personalized learning plans, a lawyer for legal research, or a chef for recipe creation. The possibilities are endless, and the key is to understand how AI can enhance, not replace, your unique human skills.

To strengthen these future-proof skills, look for opportunities to stretch yourself: join cross-functional teams, take on unfamiliar projects, or participate in workshops on communication and creative thinking (many are free at libraries or online). Leadership training isn't just for managers; anyone benefits from learning how to guide others through uncertain times.

Building this skillset not only safeguards your career, but it also attracts others to you when challenges, change, or truly open-ended problems arise.

From Fear to Fluency in Overcoming "I'm Not Technical" Objections

You might hear "I'm not a tech person" and think it's a hard stop for anything AI-related. However, that old story no longer holds. Today's AI tools are designed for regular users, not just software engineers or data scientists. Instead of cryptic command lines, you get big buttons, friendly tutorials, and natural language prompts. Take platforms like *ChatGPT* or *Canva Magic Write*, they feel more like texting a friend or dragging and dropping photos into a digital scrapbook than anything complicated. You type a question or upload a file, and the AI responds in plain English: no programming, no scary screens, no need to memorize commands. For instance, *Canva Magic Write* can help you draft professional emails or reports. At the same time, *ChatGPT* can assist in generating creative ideas or solving problems.

Non-coders are leading the charge in many workplaces. There's the office manager who set up an AI-powered scheduling assistant to wrangle meeting chaos, without writing a single script. Or the HR coordinator who uses document summarizers to review stacks of resumes in minutes. These aren't rare unicorns; they're people who got curious, clicked around, and realized that most AI tools need a little bit of exploration and a willingness to try.

To build confidence with AI tools, begin with a simple exercise. Find a free or trial version of an accessible AI app. *ChatGPT* is an easy pick, but *Canva Magic Write* or an AI email assistant also work well. Create an account using your email. Once you're in, feed it a real task: paste a chunk of messy meeting notes, then ask it to summarize the key decisions. Watch as it generates a concise list you can use. Or upload an old resume and ask for suggestions to make it more impactful. Celebrate that tiny win, now you've seen the value, not just in theory but in your world.

A lot of tech anxiety comes from feeling like you must be perfect on the first try. Instead, treat each experiment as play. What if you approached that new tool like a recipe from a cuisine you've never tried? Some ingredients may be unfamiliar, but you're just testing flavors; if it turns out weird, no harm is done. This "let's-see-what-happens" mindset opens doors instead of shutting them. Try jotting down your thoughts before and after using an AI app:

- What did you expect?

- What surprised you?

- Did anything feel easier than anticipated?

- If the answer is "yes," that's progress.

Hearing from others can help too. One librarian I spoke with had always avoided tech upgrades at work but was persuaded to pilot an AI tool for cataloging books. She watched a twenty-minute video, clicked through the setup, and ended up shaving hours off her weekly routine. Now she runs workshops for others who were once as nervous as she was. There's also the graphic designer who never coded but uses AI brainstorming tools to break creative blocks. These are real people, regular backgrounds, growing beyond their doubts.

If you want to keep learning without pressure, there are tons of free or low-risk resources out there. *Google's* "AI for Everyone" offers interactive tutorials that walk you through the basics step by step, using real-life examples instead of heavy jargon. Many local libraries and community centers host tech workshops where you get hands-on help from patient instructors (and they're usually free). Peer support groups thrive online. Search for beginner-friendly forums or social media groups where no question is too fundamental and experienced users are happy to lend a hand.

You don't have to leap into the deep end or become "the tech person" overnight. Perhaps today you set up one account and try out one feature; next week, you can compare notes with a coworker or attend a brief online session to review your progress. The key is momentum: each small step builds confidence, turning worry into curiosity and then into capability. You'll find that what once felt intimidating quickly becomes routine, sometimes even fun, when you let yourself experiment and learn at your own pace.

Learning to Collaborate with AI as a Human-in-the-Loop for Best Practices

Working alongside AI isn't just about pressing "go" on an app and hoping for the best. There's a real craft to collaborating with these tools, and it starts with a simple but powerful idea: "human-in-the-loop," or HITL. This means that you, the human, stay involved at key points, whether that's setting up the process, checking the results, or stepping in when things get complicated. HITL matters because AI, for all its speed and pattern-spotting, still misses context, gets tripped up by outliers, and sometimes spits out answers that sound convincing but are totally off base. When you stay informed, you catch things that don't add up, offer common sense, and ensure fairness isn't just a checkbox but a genuine priority.

Picture a workflow where you let AI scan daily transactions for fraud. Instead of allowing it to flag or freeze accounts on its own, you set rules: AI can auto-approve low-risk stuff, but anything odd or high-value lands in your inbox for review. You provide feedback, perhaps spotting a new scam trend or realizing that it misread a legitimate purchase. By reviewing and correcting these cases, you help the system get smarter over time. When it comes to something like medical advice or legal contracts, you want a real person to check those AI-generated outputs before acting. It's not just about catching errors; it's about protecting people from bad outcomes.

Best practices for HITL start with setting boundaries. Make clear calls about what tasks AI can handle alone and when a human needs to step in, draw a line between "recommendation" and "decision." For example, AI might suggest edits in a press release, but shouldn't publish it straight to the website. In high-stakes situations, such as patient records, legal filings, and financial approvals, humans should always review before any final action is taken. Keep a simple record of times you override the AI or spot patterns it missed; this isn't about blame, it's about learning and improving together.

Don't let automation lull you into complacency. Automation bias is real; you see an answer from a machine and assume it's right because it looks official. Resist that urge. Treat AI suggestions as just that: suggestions, not gospel. Encourage your team to review their outputs and conduct regular spot checks. If your system starts making weird decisions or performance drops, don't shrug it off, dig in and find out why.

Human-in-the-Loop Templates and Reflection Prompts

Here's a quick checklist for bringing a new AI tool into your work-flow:

- Map out which steps are automated and where a human review or approval is required.

- Define "red flag" scenarios where human review is needed (e.g., odd spending patterns, critical health alerts).

- Set up regular audits to compare decisions made by AI with those made by people.

- Create a simple override log: what was changed, why, and what the outcome was.

And here's a prompt to keep in mind: "When should I intervene?" If you ever catch yourself hesitating, maybe the answer feels strange, or the stakes are high, pause and check. If in doubt, err on the side of human judgment.

A template for documenting overrides can be as basic as a shared spreadsheet or form:

- Date

- Task/decision

- Original AI output

- Human action taken

- Reason for intervention

- Follow-up result

This habit provides a clear path for learning, helps identify recurring issues, and fosters trust with others who rely on your work. Over time, your blend of oversight and feedback helps both people and machines get better at what they do together.

Collaborating with AI should feel more like coaching a teammate than flipping on autopilot. You bring the judgment, context, and adaptability; the AI brings speed and memory. The real win comes when you strike a balance between both, knowing when to trust the system and when to trust your instincts.

A No-Nonsense Buyer's Guide to Assessing AI Products

Choosing an AI tool can often feel overwhelming; there's a lot of flashy marketing, but clarity can be hard to find. Fortunately, you don't need to be a tech expert to make a savvy decision. Utilize a straightforward framework based on key principles: transparency, tangible results, firm support, data privacy, and explainability.

- Start by checking if the company clearly describes what its AI is capable of.

- If they hide behind jargon or avoid straightforward answers, that's a red flag.

- Next, examine their track record by looking for real case studies, user testimonials, and independent reviews.

- Beware of products with only marketing claims and no proof of results.

- Support is equally essential; check whether you'll have access to helpful, human support or just be left with technical manuals.

- Insist on clarity about your data: find out exactly how it's used, accessed, stored, and whether it's shared.

- Finally, demand explainability; if the AI makes decisions for you, you should be able to ask why and get a clear, honest answer.

When you're ready to try a new tool, don't rely on glossy demos. Pilot the tool in your daily work, like a test drive. Set measurable goals upfront (e.g., cut scheduling time by 30% or flag 90% of duplicate invoices). Use the AI tool in conjunction with your current method for at least a week or two, taking notes on what works well, what needs improvement, and any issues you encounter. Involve real end users, the people who'll use it every day, who often spot the most significant problems. After your trial, gather frank feedback:

- Was anything easier or more efficient?

- What was frustrating?

- Did it save time or improve quality?

- Compare the numbers to assess the before-and-after results, such as speed, accuracy, or error rates.

Stay alert for warning signs during evaluation. Be cautious of overly ambitious promises, such as "our AI does everything" or claims that it can "replace all your staff." Such statements usually signal exaggeration. If documentation is vague or it's tough to find setup help, that's a concern. Be aware of unexpected costs; sometimes, features you thought were standard may require additional payments after the free trial period. Additionally, if there are no independent reviews or references (only glowing testimonials on the company's website), exercise caution.

Printable Buyer's Checklist and Sample Questions

Here's a checklist you can use when assessing any new AI product:

- Can the vendor clearly explain what their AI does and how it works, without using jargon?

- Are real-world case studies or independent reviews available (not just their testimonials)?

- What support options are offered? (Live chat, phone, email?) Is it included in the price?

- How is your data collected, stored, used, and deleted? Is it shared with external parties?

- Can the company demonstrate how its AI makes decisions, using examples?

- What's the data export process if you leave? Is it easy to extract your data?

- Are all features included in the listed price? Any fees after a free trial?

- How frequently are updates released? Is there a straightforward way to report issues or suggest features?

Sample questions for your vendor:

- "How is my data used and stored? Who has access?"

- "Can you explain how the AI works in real-world use?"

- "What support do you provide if I need help?"

- "Is there a free trial so I can compare the tool to my current system?"

- "Who in my industry is using this? Can I speak to current users?"

If a vendor avoids these questions or provides only vague responses, trust your instincts and look elsewhere. Asking clear, tough questions upfront saves you trouble later.

Next Steps for Work and Life in Building Your Personal AI Action Plan

It's easy to look at all the AI options out there and feel paralyzed by choice, but making progress is simpler when you zoom in on what matters most in your day-to-day activities. Grab a notepad, your phone's notes app, or a big sticky note - whatever works. Start by jotting down where you spend most of your time, both at work and at home. Which tasks drain your energy? Perhaps it's endless scheduling, sifting through emails, chasing reminders, or simply keeping up with reading. As you review your list, circle one or two areas where you think a little automation could give you some breathing room. This isn't about overhauling everything overnight. It's about targeting easy wins, low-risk, and high-reward spots that let you dip your toes in without drama.

Now, take a close look at your strengths and areas for improvement. Are you great at brainstorming but struggle with note-taking? Perhaps you excel at big-picture creative work but spend hours researching or sorting files. Maybe you're organized but want to free up time to focus on learning or mentoring others. Identify one gap that frustrates you most and one area where a little extra support could make your life noticeably better.

Once you've identified those gaps, select a single AI tool or project to try, one with a gentle learning curve and clear value. If your calendar is chaotic, try an AI scheduling assistant that integrates with your existing tools. If writing takes a long time, consider using an AI-powered outline creator or document summarizer to streamline the process.

The trick is to pick one thing that already has a free trial or a no-cost version. Commit to using it for two weeks and see how it feels in your real workflow.

Setting a goal helps keep things moving forward. Make it SMART: Specific, Measurable, Achievable, Relevant, and Time-bound. Instead of "I want to use more AI," pin down something like: "In the next month, I'll use an AI notetaker for all team meetings and experiment with one creative AI tool for personal projects." You'll know exactly what success looks like and how much effort it will take. Keep your goals practical; there's no prize for picking ten tools and burning out after a week.

Tracking progress doesn't have to mean elaborate spreadsheets, though; if you love those, go for it. For most people, a digital journal, a simple spreadsheet, or even just a recurring calendar reminder works fine. After each week, jot down what went well, what surprised you, and what felt clunky. If you're comfortable, share these updates with a friend or coworker who's also exploring AI; peer accountability makes it easier to keep going and can spark new ideas when you hit a wall.

Don't underestimate the power of celebrating small wins along the way. Every time an AI tool saves you twenty minutes or solves a nagging problem, add it to a "wins" board, physical or digital. These little victories add up fast and keep motivation high. If you're feeling brave, post about your progress on *LinkedIn* or another social platform (even if you're sharing lessons learned with colleagues). You might be surprised by who chimes in with encouragement or swaps their tips.

Your Next Step

Take fifteen minutes this week for a quick self-audit:

- What's the one task I most want to automate or simplify?

- Which AI tool seems like the best candidate for that job?

- What's my SMART goal for the next 30 days?

- How will I track my progress and reflect on what I learn?

- Who can I share my results with for feedback or to celebrate?

Tackling AI doesn't have to mean becoming an overnight expert or reworking your entire routine. Instead, it's about small bets, one experiment at a time, that build real momentum. As you try new tools and document what helps, you'll start spotting more opportunities and feel less overwhelmed by the noise. Every little step counts.

Educating and Advocating in Your Community by Becoming an AI Ambassador

I suspect at some point you've explained a tricky app to a friend or helped a parent figure out their phone. In that case, you're already halfway to being an AI ambassador. The best ambassadors aren't the loudest in the room or the most technical; they're the people who approach new ideas with curiosity, ask honest questions, and listen before jumping to conclusions. It takes humility to admit you don't know everything, especially when technology advances at such a rapid pace. But that very quality makes your voice relatable and trustworthy. When you break down a complicated AI topic for someone, translating tech-speak into plain language or using real-life examples, you make it less intimidating. For instance, instead of diving into the mechanics of machine learning, you might say, "It's like your streaming service guessing what movies you'll like based on what you've watched." Your goal isn't to show off knowledge; it's to help others feel included.

Starting conversations about AI doesn't have to mean giving a lecture or writing a lengthy report; it can be as simple as sharing a relevant article or a thought-provoking quote. Small actions pack a punch. Hosting a "lunch and learn" session at work is a great way to introduce colleagues to new tools or trends in a casual setting. You could bring snacks, show a short video, and then discuss how AI might save time or reduce stress in your office routines. In your neighborhood or online circles, consider organizing a book club or discussion group centered around an article or podcast episode that explores the role of AI in daily life. Keep it friendly, open, and free from jargon. Sometimes, all it takes is writing a simple blog post or social media update explaining how you used an AI app to solve a real problem. Your story becomes an invitation for others to try it too.

When people raise doubts or express anxiety about AI, don't dismiss their concerns. Instead, invite open conversation and meet skepticism with facts and understanding. I like to use myth-versus-reality callouts, perhaps on a handout or in an email, to distinguish between rumors and what's happening. For example, someone might worry that AI will put everyone out of work overnight. You can share evidence that while some tasks change, new roles and opportunities are constantly emerging. Balanced perspectives matter; avoid hype and also avoid doom-and-gloom predictions. Listen carefully, repeat back what you hear, and provide examples that show AI's strengths and its limits.

There are so many ways to make a difference beyond your immediate group. Schools, libraries, and local nonprofits often seek volunteers who can help demystify digital technology. You might partner with a teacher to lead an after-school workshop about how search engines use AI, or help library patrons spot fake news generated by bots. Digital inclusion programs require ambassadors who can guide seniors or newcomers through the safe and responsible use of AI; sometimes, all it takes is patience and a good sense of humor. If you enjoy creating resources, think about building short guides or cheat sheets that walk people through the basics: "How to spot AI-generated content," "Five safe ways to try AI at home," or even "What does 'algorithm' mean?" Share these with your network, print them for local bulletin boards, or post them online.

As an AI ambassador, you don't need all the answers. What matters is your willingness to learn alongside others, admit when things are unclear, and ask thoughtful questions. You build bridges between technology and people's everyday experiences, making sure nobody feels left behind. The most powerful impact often comes from small moments, a reassuring conversation in the break room, an encouraging comment on someone's first attempt with a new tool, or the relief on someone's face when they finally "get it." Over time, these small efforts accumulate and ripple outward.

In wrapping up this chapter, remember: being an AI ambassador isn't about expertise, it's about empathy, clear communication, and inviting others to grow with you. When you help those around you understand and use AI thoughtfully, you strengthen your community against both fear and hype. These connections will matter even more as technology continues to evolve. Now, as we move forward, let's explore practical ways to support broader digital inclusion and ensure that everyone has a fair chance at thriving in this changing world.

Conclusion

I f you've made it this far, take a minute to pat yourself on the back. Seriously. You've powered through a topic that's confusing, hyped, and sometimes downright intimidating. You've done the hard part: showing up, staying curious, and letting yourself imagine what's possible when you turn AI into your assistant instead of something to fear.

Take a moment to appreciate how far you've come. When we started, AI may have seemed like a daunting black box, with buzzwords and headlines creating a cloud of confusion. But you've made significant strides. I aimed to demystify AI, simplify the jargon, and make it a practical tool for you to use. Together, we've dismantled the mystery surrounding AI, understanding what it truly is, how it 'learns,' and why it's more of a helpful sidekick than a sci-fi villain.

We walked through plain-language explanations of machine learning, deep learning, and those legendary large language models. You got real-world examples, no code, no math degree required. Then, we rolled up our sleeves and explored practical tools: AI that keeps your calendar on track, sorts your email, helps with research, and even finds the best deals when you're shopping. We examined how AI is assisting parents, educators, business owners, and professionals across various industries. Regardless of your background or career stage, you've discovered a toolkit for saving time, reducing stress, and accomplishing tasks more efficiently.

But we didn't just talk gadgets and shortcuts. We also tackled the challenging topics, including ethics, bias, and privacy. You learned how to spot when an algorithm might be unfair, what to look for in privacy policies, and why "human-in-the-loop" isn't just a buzzword but a fundamental safeguard for your decisions. We discussed AI's emotional blind spots, why empathy still belongs to humans, and how to combine the speed of machines with the wisdom and care that only people can provide.

You've gained not only knowledge but also practical strategies for every aspect of your life and work. We've covered the basics, how AI 'thinks' and learns. Then we moved on to daily routines, showing how AI can serve as your calendar concierge, research assistant, and even a creative partner. We've delved into sector blueprints, healthcare, finance, manufacturing, and education, so you can see where this technology is already making a difference (and where it still needs a human touch). For business owners and leaders, we've provided step-by-step adoption guides, vendor checklists, and simple ways to launch your first pilot without hiring a team of programmers. You're not just informed; you're capable.

And you didn't just learn what to do. You learned how to keep learning. From newsletters to mind maps, curated toolkits to online communities, you now have a roadmap for staying up to date, without drowning in information overload or shiny new apps. You know how to spot hype, ask good questions, and keep your toolkit lean and functional.

Most importantly, you have the tools and confidence to not just keep up with AI but to shape how you use it. You can pick and test tools that solve your problems, rather than just adding more clutter. You can check for bias, demand transparency, and ensure your data (and your privacy) remains protected. You know when to trust the machine, and when to ask for a second opinion or escalate to a real person.

If you're reading this, you've already taken a huge step. You've reduced confusion and built a foundation for lifelong learning with AI. You've demonstrated that you're ready for change, and you're not going to sit back while the future unfolds without you. You're going to be part of it.

So, what's next? My challenge to you: Pick one new AI tool from this book and try it this week. Maybe it's an AI notetaker like *Otter.ai* for your next meeting, a smart to-do app like *Todoist*, or a research assistant like *Miro* to help you plan your next vacation. Set a small, clear goal: "I'll use this AI tool every day for the next two weeks and track what changes." Please keep it simple and doable.

And remember, you're not alone in this journey. Share your wins, your questions, and your roadblocks. You'll find that there are many people like you, curious, a little skeptical, and eager to make sense of all this new technology. That's how we all get better, together. You're part of a supportive community, always ready to help.

Here's something even bigger: become an AI ambassador. You don't need to be a tech expert to help friends, family, or coworkers take their first steps. Share what you've learned. Hold a mini-workshop, write a helpful post, or offer to walk someone through setting up a new tool. When you hear someone repeat an AI myth or worry about being "left behind," you can offer facts, empathy, and maybe even a little inspiration.

Remember, AI will keep changing. Tools will come and go. Headlines will swing from doom to hype and back again. But you've built a toolkit that lasts: curiosity, ethical thinking, practical skills, and the willingness to try, learn, and adapt. When you encounter a snag or feel overwhelmed, return to these pages, the digital resources, or an online community for support. You've got this.

I wrote this book because, like you, I was tired of feeling overwhelmed and left out by new technology. I wanted something honest, helpful, and grounded in real life. I hope you feel more confident, more informed, and better equipped to use AI as your assistant, both at home and at work, wherever life takes you.

Here's my final wish for you: Stay open, stay ethical, and keep sharing what you learn. The future isn't something that happens to us; it's something that we create. It's something we shape, one wise, responsible, human-centered decision at a time. You don't need to be perfect. You need to start. And you already have. Remember, ethical use of AI is not just a choice, it's a responsibility. Let's ensure we utilize this powerful tool for the betterment of all.

For more people to benefit from the information in this book, they need your help. If this book was informative and of use to you, please leave an honest review to help others recognize this resource.

Thank you,
George Munson

References

- abhinav.japesh@superagi. (2025, June 27). Top 10 AI lead Scoring Tools of 2025: A Comprehensive Comparison and review - SuperAGI. SuperAGI. https://superagi.com/top-10-ai-lead-scoring-tools-of-2025-a-comprehensive-comparison-and-review-5/

- AI Imaging & Diagnostics - Google for Health. (n.d.). https://health.google/intl/en_id/health-research/imaging-and-diagnostics/

- AI Readiness Checklist for SMBs | Acumatica Cloud ERP. (2025, July 21). Acumatica Cloud ERP. https://www.acumatica.com/ai-readiness-evaluation-checklist/

- Bennett, M. (2024, October 7). Artificial intelligence vs. human intelligence: Differences explained. Search Enterprise AI. https://www.techtarget.com/searchenterpriseai/tip/Artificial-intelligence-vs-human-intelligence-How-are-they-different

- ByteBridge. (2025, February 16). Comparing leading AI

deep research tools: ChatGPT, Google, Perplexity, Kompas AI, and Elicit. Medium. https://bytebridge.medium.com/comparing-leading-ai-deep-research-tools-chatgpt-google-perplexity-kompas-ai-and-elicit-59678c511f18

• Chrome Music Lab. (n.d.). https://musiclab.chromeexperiments.com/

• Document AI security and compliance. (n.d.). Google Cloud. https://cloud.google.com/document-ai/docs/security

• Everyday examples and applications of artificial intelligence (AI). (n.d.). Tableau. https://www.tableau.com/data-insights/ai/examples

• Jin, W., Fan, J., Gromala, D., Pasquier, P., & Hamarneh, G. (2021, February 4). EUCA: the End-User-Centered Explainable AI Framework. arXiv.org. https://arxiv.org/abs/2102.02437

• Kennedy, R. (2024, October 22). Council Post: 10 considerations when Evaluating an AI Tool. Forbes. https://www.forbes.com/councils/forbestechcouncil/2024/10/22/10-considerations-when-evaluating-an-ai-tool/

• Less_Code. (2024, December 31). Top No-Code AI Tools of 2025: In-Depth Guide — BuildFire. Buildfire. https://buildfire.com/no-code-ai-tools/

• MyStudyLife. (2024, May 20). Top 10 AI tools for Homework: Best apps and websites. mystudylife. https://mystud

ylife.com/ai-tools-for-homework/

- Qu, Y., & Wang, J. (2024). Performance and biases of Large Language Models in public opinion simulation. Humanities and Social Sciences Communications, 11(1). https://doi.o rg/10.1057/s41599-024-03609-x

- Revolutionizing Industries: AI-Driven case studies and success stories in Real-World applications and innovations. (2024, July 4). IEEE Conference Publication | IEEE Xplore. https://ieeexplore.ieee.org/document/10866349/

- Ryseff, J., F, D. B. B., & Newberry, S. J. (2024, August 13). The root causes of failure for artificial intelligence projects and how they can succeed: Avoiding the Anti-Patterns of AI. RAND. https://www.rand.org/pubs/research_reports /RRA2680-1.html

- SKAI | WFP Innovation. (n.d.). https://innovation.wfp.or g/project/SKAI

- Team, I. D. a. A. (2025, June 4). AI vs. Machine Learning vs. Deep Learning vs. Neural Networks. IBM. https://www.ibm.com/think/topics/ai-vs-machine-l earning-vs-deep-learning-vs-neural-networks

- The 10 Best AI Resume Builders for 2025 (Tested & Reviewed). (2025, July 7). MyPerfectResume. https://www.myperfectresume.com/career-center/r esumes/basics/ai-resume-builder

- Using AI to improve your health. (n.d.) . https://www.texashealth.org/areyouawellbeing/Health-a

nd-Well-Being/Using-AI-to-Improve-Your-Health

- What do you do if you want to learn AI as a beginner? (2024, March 20). https://www.linkedin.com/advice/1/what-do-you-want-learn-ai-beginner-skills-artificial-intelligence-ozd0f